Great Writing 1

Great Sentences for Great Paragraphs

Great Writing 1

Great Sentences for Great Paragraphs

THIRD EDITION

KEITH S. FOLSE
UNIVERSITY OF CENTRAL FLORIDA

APRIL MUCHMORE-VOKOUN
HILLSBOROUGH COMMUNITY COLLEGE

ELENA VESTRI SOLOMON
EMIRATES COLLEGE FOR ADVANCED EDUCATION
UAE

HEINLE
CENGAGE Learning™

Australia • Canada • Mexico • Singapore • Spain • United Kingdom • United States

HEINLE
CENGAGE Learning

Great Writing 1: Great Sentences for Great Paragraphs
Keith S. Folse, April Muchmore-Vokoun, Elena Vestri Solomon

Publisher: Sherrise Roehr

Acquisition Editor: Tom Jefferies

Senior Development Editor: Yeny Kim

Assistant Editor: Marissa Petrarca

Director of Content and Media Production: Michael Burggren

Marketing Director, U.S.: Jim McDonough

Director of Adult Education Sales: Eric Bredenberg

Marketing Communications Manager: Beth Leonard

Senior Product Marketing Manager: Katie Kelley

Academic Marketing Manager: Caitlin Driscoll

Senior Content Project Manager: Maryellen Eschmann-Killeen

Senior Print Buyer: Susan Spencer

Composition: Pre-Press PMG

Library of Congress Control Number: 2007922480

ISBN-13: 978-1-4240-4989-9

ISBN-10: 1-4240-4989-X

Heinle
20 Channel Center Street
Boston, MA 02210
USA

Cengage learning is a leading provider of customized learning solutions with office locations around the globe, including Singapore, the United Kingdom, Australia, Mexico, Brazil, and Japan. Locate our local office at **www.cengage.com/global**

Cengage Learning products are represented in Canada by Nelson Education, Ltd.

Visit Heinle online at **elt.heinle.com**
Visit our corporate website at **cengage.com**

Printed in the United States of America
2 3 4 5 6 7 14 13 12 11 10

Contents

Overview

Great Writing 1: Great Sentences for Great Paragraphs is the first book in the five-level *Great Writing* series of composition books. In *Great Writing 1*, students become better writers by focusing their attention on the elements of writing a good sentence within simple paragraphs. This book provides practice that helps students not only to understand the writing process, but also to produce a correctly written final product.

The book is designed for students who are novice writers. It is especially suited for beginning to lower intermediate students but may be used with any level writer who is unfamiliar with the basics of writing correct sentences in simple paragraphs. Depending on the class level and the amount of writing that is done outside of class, there is enough material for 60 to 80 classroom hours. If more of the writing is done outside of class, the number of hours for a faster group can be as few as 40.

Some of the highlights of *Great Writing 1* include the following:

- **Abundance of activities and writing practice** There are 204 activities, including at least 70 suggestions for additional writing and 10 extra writing activities in Appendix 2 for students who need additional help or practice. New to this edition, the Timed Writing feature provides students with an opportunity to practice writing using a writing prompt with a time limit.

- **Step-by-step instruction** Some English learners are already good writers in their native language, but others need work in the basic steps involved in the process of composing sentences and paragraphs. These students in particular will benefit from the guidance that the step-by-step instruction provides in the unit activities, as well as in the Appendices. Of special interest are Appendix 1, Building Better Sentences, which contains guided activities to improve students' sentence combination skills, and the new Editing Your Writing section of the Brief Writer's Handbook, which provides a step-by-step introduction to the process of identifying and correcting errors and rewriting drafts based on teacher feedback.

- **Contextualized activities** A very important feature of *Great Writing 1* is the inclusion of 96 example paragraphs distributed throughout the units. Instead of exercises consisting of unrelated sentences, most of the activities in this book present whole paragraphs of related sentences on a single topic. In addition to providing relevant practice on some aspect of the sentence, these contextualized activities provide learners with more input in English composition and serve as models in paragraph organization and cohesion.

- **Enhanced focus on vocabulary** A piece of writing is often only as good as the writer's ability to use a wide range of appropriate vocabulary. To help our learners achieve this important goal of having an increased vocabulary, this third edition includes more emphasis on vocabulary in four key ways:

  1. *More recycling.* We have intentionally recycled vocabulary items from unit to unit. With increased exposure, students will learn not only the basic meanings of words and phrases, but also acquire actual natural usage.

  2. *Practice of meaning.* Each unit contains a Word Associations activity that allows students to check their understanding of the basic meaning of new vocabulary.

3. *Practice of collocations.* Each unit also includes an activity on collocations, which are words or groups of words that naturally and frequently co-occur with a target word. Learning collocations will help students build on their bank of commonly used phrases, which is the first step to incorporating those phrases into their writing.

4. *Active use of vocabulary.* While knowing word meanings may allow for passive recognition in reading or listening, knowledge of word meanings alone is often insufficient for using the vocabulary accurately and fluently in writing (or speaking). Students need to practice the vocabulary items and collocations presented in these activities in their writing. To this end, students are instructed to use some of the vocabulary presented in the vocabulary activities as they write their Original Writing Practice assignment for that unit.

The teacher is always the best judge of which units and which activities should be covered with any group of students. It is up to you to gauge the needs of your students and then match those needs with the material in this book.

Text Organization

Units 1–8

Great Writing 1 consists of eight units. Unit 1 and Units 3 through 7 deal with a particular aspect of writing correct sentences in simple paragraphs. Unit 2 introduces students to the basic elements of a paragraph and asks students to analyze these elements. Unit 8 contains an additional 27 writing activities.

In Unit 1, students learn the basic parts of a sentence. Students learn the importance of subjects and verbs in a sentence.

In Unit 2, students see the connection between sentences and paragraphs. Novice writers learn the basic parts of a paragraph and how their sentences can fit into these parts.

In Unit 3, students write about the present. They practice writing sentences using the simple present tense.

In Unit 4, students write about the past. Here students practice the simple past tense of both regular and irregular verbs.

In Unit 5, students practice describing actions. The writing activities in this unit guide students through the use of the present progressive (continuous) tense to accomplish this.

In Unit 6, students write about the future. They have numerous opportunities to use *will* and *be + going to* in their writing and to compare this to the tenses that they have learned in previous units of this book.

Unit 7 offers a more difficult but necessary lesson in writing. Here students learn to build better sentences by using adjective clauses in their writing. Students learn not only the structure of these clauses but also their correct placement within sentences.

Unit 8 consists of 27 activities that provide further guided and free practice of the techniques presented in this text. These activities may be done toward the end of the course, or they may be done while the students are still working in the first seven units of the book. In addition, these activities may be used as remedial help for weaker students or for bonus work for students who have already finished the work in the first seven units. As this is a bonus unit, it only contains basic vocabulary building activities.

Brief Writer's Handbook

The Brief Writer's Handbook offers instruction in a wide array of basic writing areas, including a verb tense overview, capitalization, spelling rules for adding *-ed*, irregular past tense, spelling rules for adding *-ing*, stative verbs, the definite article *the*, non-count nouns, possessive adjectives, quantifiers, prepositions, comma rules, order of adjectives, connectors, and definitions of useful language terms. The material is presented in a very simple and clear manner and is accompanied by pertinent examples.

The Handbook includes the new Editing Your Writing section. Teachers often spend considerable time marking and commenting on student work, but many students have difficulty incorporating teacher feedback as they write their next draft. While this innovative section is meant to provide students with the training they need to appropriately integrate teacher feedback and serves as a guided introduction to the editing process. In Editing Your Writing, students analyze three versions of the same student paragraph.

- Version 1 is an uncorrected draft of a student-generated, timed-writing assignment. Students read the assigned writing task and then the original paragraph to compare the task and the product globally. Students then read the paragraph for a closer inspection of the organization, grammar, vocabulary, and writing style.

- Version 2 is the same paragraph with instructor comments. In this version, students can see what the instructor has written. Students will see both positive and negative comments. An important point here is for students to compare their comments after reading Version 1 with the teacher's comments. Which comments are similar? Which areas are different?

- Version 3 is the second draft of the work after the teacher's comments. The writer has accepted some of the teacher's comments but appears to have rejected others, which is a very common occurrence in all composition classes. Through guided questions, students are asked to identify sections that were changed. Were the changes made in response to teacher comments, or were the changes original changes initiated by the student?

While many textbooks offer general advice on editing, students often need more specific and explicit advice. Editing Your Writing provides students with guided, step-by-step instruction on how to effectively use teacher comments to improve their writing.

Appendices

Appendix 1, Building Better Sentences, consists of twenty-two exercises that help students build better sentences in English through sentence combining. Some students' writing contains many simple sentences that barely go beyond subject-verb-object or subject-*be*-adjective constructions. While such sentences may be correct, this type of writing lacks variety and appears very simplistic. Instructing students to write longer sentences may help them write more. However, it is guided practice with creating compound and complex sentences that will help students write *better* and that is the key to advancing the writing skills of students at this level. Teaching and practicing this sentence variety are essential components of a good writing course at this level. To this end, we have provided twenty-two practice activities aptly called Building Better Sentences. A real advantage of these activities from the teacher's point of view is that these activities can be checked as a whole class, thereby reducing teacher grading time.

Appendix 2 is a collection of ten guided paragraph activities. Many of these activities require students to read and study short paragraphs, make a series of basic changes, and then rewrite their new paragraph. Other activities are more open-ended. These activities are designed to be done as additional work to support or supplement the material within the main units of the book.

Appendix 3 consists of the peer editing sheets for the peer editing activity in each unit. While we believe that the best way to learn to edit is to practice editing, we believe that lower-level students in particular should not edit written work without the kind of guidance (i.e., teaching) that is provided by these peer editing sheets.

The Answer Key and additional practices can be found on the *Great Writing 1* Web site: elt.heinle.com/greatwriting.

Contents of a Unit

Though each unit has a specific writing goal and Grammar and Sentence Structure, the following features appear in almost every unit.

Timed Writing

One way to improve students' comfort level with the task of writing under a deadline, such as during a testing situation, is to provide them with numerous writing opportunities that are timed. As a result, in this third edition, Units 3-7 provide students with a timed writing prompt that is geared toward the Grammar and Sentence Structure presented in each unit. This assignment can be done alone or in conjunction with the editing approach introduced in the Editing Your Work section of the Brief Writer's Handbook.

Although we have placed this Timed Writing as a final task within a unit, some teachers may prefer to assign this topic as the first task of the unit. In this case, these teachers usually collect students' work and then have them rewrite it at the end of the unit. In this way, students have two opportunities to practice composition while teachers only read and mark papers once.

Grammar and Sentence Structure

One of the biggest problems for many beginning (and even advanced) writers is grammar. While nonnative speakers will always make some errors, it is important to help students realize what their major grammar and sentence structure problems are and then to provide appropriate instructions and practice exercises and activities.

The grammar and sentence structure points are language structures that are necessary to complete the writing tasks within that unit. For example, in Unit 5, Describing Actions, students are asked to pay particular attention to the use of verbs in the present progressive (continuous) tense because this language structure is necessary to write descriptions of actions. Likewise, in Unit 7, students are taught to build up sentence variety through the use of adjective clauses. Students first learn about adjective clauses but are then asked to produce sentences and then small paragraphs that incorporate this sentence structure.

Sentence Development

One of the main goals of *Great Writing 1* is for students to learn the basics of the simple sentence in English. However, an equally important and related goal is for students to move beyond the simple sentence and begin including compound and complex sentences in their original writing. Thus, this section provides important practice in helping students expand their repertoire of sentence structures in English.

Writer's Notes

Rather than large boxed areas overflowing with information, *Great Writing 1* features small chunks of writing advice under this heading. The content of these writer's notes varies from brainstorming techniques, peer editing guidelines, and journal writing advice to correct comma usage.

Building Better Sentences

At the end of the unit, students are asked to turn to Appendix 1 and work on building better sentences. This activity focuses on students' sentence-level writing skills. For those students who lack confidence in producing longer or more complicated sentences, this type of activity concentrates on the manipulations of words and ideas at the sentence level.

Building Better Vocabulary

Before the Original Writing Practice in every unit, students will complete three separate vocabulary-building activities. In these activities, vocabulary words have been taken from each unit's writing, and special attention is paid to building schema, collocations, and parts of speech. In the first activity, Word Associations, students identify words that best relate to the target vocabulary word. This allows them to build connections to more words and thus grow their vocabulary more quickly. The second activity, Using Collocations, builds students' understanding that some words typically appear in conjunction with a certain word and helps students learn these specific word combinations, or collocations. In the final activity, Parts of Speech, students study affixes and parts of speech. Understanding how affixes are related to the different parts of speech allows students to expand their understanding of word formation in English, giving them a broader vocabulary base and a better understanding of word order for better writing skills.

Editing

Teaching students to edit their own writing is one of the most important goals of any writing course. To this end, *Great Writing 1* provides several types of editing practice and activities throughout the units.

Guided Writing Practice

Because of the lower proficiency of students using this book, guided writing practice activities are included. In the more basic exercises, students are asked to copy a paragraph and make only four or five rather simple changes. Eventually, the changes become more complicated. While the students are not writing original work here, they are gaining critical confidence with the conventions of good writing, such as the use of capital letters, indenting, handwriting (or typing), and punctuation.

Peer Editing

Each unit contains an activity in which a student trades papers with another student and then makes comments about the partner's paper. Because of the lower proficiency level of the students, it is especially important to provide novice writers and editors with detailed guidelines about what to look for when editing or reviewing someone's work. Unit 1 explains what to keep in mind when reviewing someone else's work, and the Peer Editing Sheets in Appendix 3 provide the guidance and structure that is necessary for students at this level.

Journal Writing

One of the best ways to learn to write is by writing. Journal writing offers a happy compromise between informal letter (or e-mail) writing to friends and formal paragraph or essay writing. Journal writing encourages students to write about topics that they are interested in. To this end, each unit has a list of ten possible journal topics with a series of questions to encourage original student writing. These topics may be developed into class assignments, but since students' purposes for learning to write in English can vary so much, we leave the topics and parameters for course writing up to the individual instructor.

About the Activities and Practices

Teachers have long noticed that although students do well with grammar in discrete sentences, they have problems with the same grammar when it occurs in a paragraph. Because of this difficulty, most of the activities and practices in *Great Writing 1* work with complete paragraphs. Thus, instead of five unrelated sentences for practice with the past tense, we offer a paragraph of five related sentences. Our hope is that by practicing the grammatical structure within the target medium, students will produce more accurate writing sooner. The large number of such paragraphs (96) allows a great deal of freedom on the teacher's part in planning this course.

The earliest ESL composition textbooks were merely extensions of ESL grammar classes. The activities in these books did not practice English composition as much as they did ESL grammar points. Later books, on the other hand, tended to focus too much on the composing process. We feel that this process ignores the important fact that the real goal for English learners is both to produce a presentable product and to understand the composing practice. From our years of ESL and other L2 teaching experience, we believe that *Great Writing 1* allows students to achieve this goal.

For the answer key, additional exercises, and other instructor resources, visit the *Great Writing 1* instructor Web site at elt.heinle.com/greatwriting

Additional exercises for each unit are available to students on the *Great Writing 1* student Web site at elt.heinle.com/greatwriting

Acknowledgments

We would like to thank the hundreds of ESL and English composition colleagues who have generously shared their ideas, insights, and feedback on L2 writing, university English course requirements, and textbook design at conferences or in e-mail correspondence since we started writing the first edition of this series. In addition, we would like to thank teachers on two electronic lists, TESL-L and TESLIE-L, who responded to our original queries about their composition classes and thereby helped us write this book.

We would like to thank our editors at Heinle/Cengage Learning, Thomas Jefferies and Yeny Kim. We also remain forever grateful to our previous editors at Houghton Mifflin, Susan Maguire, Kathy Sands-Boehmer, and Kathleen Smith, for their indispensable guidance throughout the birth and growth of this writing project. In addition, we would like to thank our development editor, BJ Wells of Modesto Junior College, for her valuable insights and help during the editing of the second edition.

Likewise, we are indebted to the following reviewers who offered ideas and suggestions that shaped our revisions:

Don Beck, The University of Findlay, OH
Jodi Brinkley, Florida Community College, FL
Lee Chen, Palomar College, CA
Chip DiMarco, Harvard University, MA
Kathy Flynn, Glendale Community College, CA
Rebecca Ford, Sacramento City College, CA
Linda Forse, University of Texas, Brownsville, TX
Rachel Gader, Georgetown University, Washington, DC
Janet Goldstein, Bramson ORT Technological Institute, NY
Gretchen Hack, Community College of Denver, CO
Kathy Judd, Truman College, IL
Meridith Kemper, University of Central Arkansas, AR
Sarah Mitchell Kim, Miramar College, CA
Tom Kitchens, Texas Intensive English Program, Austin, TX
Chouaib Naamad, Northeastern University, MA
Nelson Rivera Agosto, University of Puerto Rico, Arecibo
Phyllis Ruppert, Coe College, IA
Kim Sanabria, Columbia University, NY
Virginia Scales, San Jose City College, CA
Ken Szok, Mt. San Antonio College, CA
Carol Thurston, Northern Virginia Community College, VA
Colleen Weldele, Palomar College, CA
Sherry Wickham, Brookhaven College, TX

Finally, many thanks go to our students who have taught us what ESL composition ought to be. Without them, this work would have been impossible.

Keith S. Folse
April Muchmore-Vokoun
Elena Vestri Solomon

Guided Tour

✳ NEW TO THIS EDITION

A new **four-color design** allows for engaging, easy-to-follow lessons.

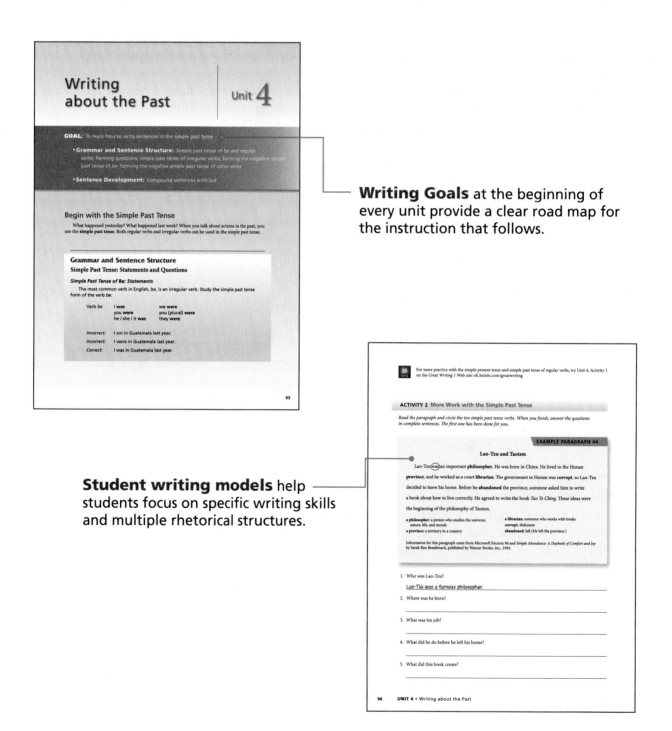

Writing Goals at the beginning of every unit provide a clear road map for the instruction that follows.

Student writing models help students focus on specific writing skills and multiple rhetorical structures.

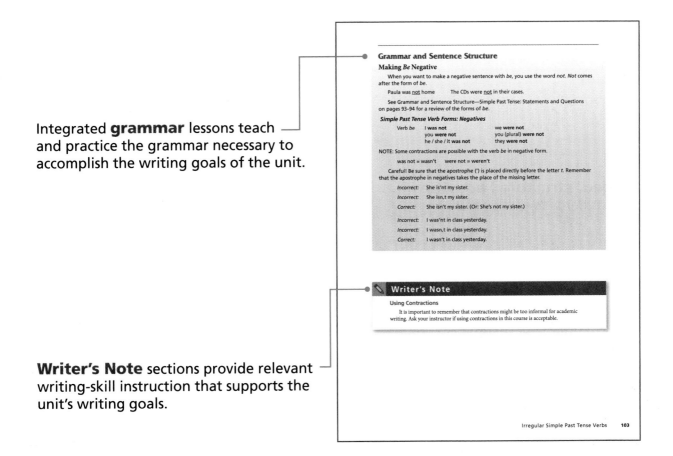

Grammar and Sentence Structure

Using Modals to Add Meaning

Writers use **modals** to add extra information to the main verb in the sentence. The modal comes before the main verb, and the main verb is always in its base form. Add *not* after the modal to make it negative. Each modal has a different meaning. Below are some common modals, their meanings, and some example sentences.

Modal	Meaning	Example Sentence
will	to show the future	Next week, Rachel **will travel** to the Ivory Coast.
should	to give advice	It is going to rain. You **should take** an umbrella.
must	to show necessity	You **must have** a visa to visit that country.
might	to show possibility	The weather is good. We **might go** to the beach.
can	to show ability	Roberto **can speak** three languages.

Remember that you cannot use two modals together. For example:

Incorrect: We might can go to a new restaurant for dinner.

Correct: We might go to a new restaurant for dinner.

Do not use the word *to* between the modal and the verb.

Incorrect: We might to play football tomorrow.

Correct: We might play football tomorrow.

Incorrect: Can you to help us with this electricity bill?

Correct: Can you help us with this electricity bill?

Yes/No *Questions*

Modal	+	Subject	+	Main Verb (base form)	+	Other Parts
Will		you		stop		at the store for me?
Should		I		call		my parents tonight?
Must		we		go		to the party? (formal and implies a complaint)
Can		they		drive		us to work?

NOTE: *Might* is rarely used in question form in American English.

Clear **Grammar Charts** visually represent the grammar taught in the unit.

Grammar and Sentence Structure

Making *Be* Negative

When you want to make a negative sentence with *be*, you use the word *not*. *Not* comes after the form of *be*.

Paula was <u>not</u> home   The CDs were <u>not</u> in their cases.

See Grammar and Sentence Structure—Simple Past Tense: Statements and Questions on pages 93–94 for a review of the forms of *be*.

Simple Past Tense Verb Forms: Negatives

Verb *be*	I was not	we were not
	you were not	you (plural) were not
	he / she / it was not	they were not

NOTE: Some contractions are possible with the verb *be* in negative form.

was not = wasn't   were not = weren't

Careful! Be sure that the apostrophe (') is placed directly before the letter *t*. Remember that the apostrophe in negatives takes the place of the missing letter.

Incorrect: She is'nt my sister.

Incorrect: She isn,t my sister.

Correct: She isn't my sister. (Or: She's not my sister.)

Incorrect: I was'nt in class yesterday.

Incorrect: I wasn,t in class yesterday.

Correct: I wasn't in class yesterday.

Integrated **grammar** lessons teach and practice the grammar necessary to accomplish the writing goals of the unit.

Writer's Note

Using Contractions

It is important to remember that contractions might be too informal for academic writing. Ask your instructor if using contractions in this course is acceptable.

Writer's Note sections provide relevant writing-skill instruction that supports the unit's writing goals.

Building Better Sentences

Correct and varied sentence structure is essential to the quality of your writing. For further practice with the sentences and paragraphs in this unit, go to Practice 4 on page 235 in Appendix 1.

Building Better Vocabulary

ACTIVITY 16 Word Associations

Circle the word or phrase that is most closely related to the word or phrase on the left. If necessary, use a dictionary to check the meaning of words you do not know.

1. horrible	very bad news	very good news
2. century	ten years	one hundred years
3. to communicate	to share information	to keep information
4. excellent	the worst	the best
5. to continue	to pause	to not stop
6. proud	grade of 45%	grade of 100%
7. province	region	project
8. librarian	books	cars
9. separate	together	apart
10. to graduate	to complete work	to complete school
11. beginning	initial	final
12. manager	boss	teacher
13. original	a copy	not a copy
14. to arrive	to come to a place	to leave a place
15. to scare	to laugh	to scream

✳ NEW TO THIS EDITION

Building Better Vocabulary features teach students how to accurately and effectively use written English.

Original Student Writing

ACTIVITY 19 Original Writing Practice

Reread the paragraph about Lao-Tzu on page 96 and your answers to Activity 3 on page 97. You will use this kind of information to write in the simple past tense about an important person.

Think of an important person. Then follow these steps for writing. Put a check (✓) next to each step as you complete it. When you finish your paragraph, use the checklist that follows to edit your work. Remember to write in the simple past tense. You may want to review What Is a Paragraph? in Unit 2 on page 39.

Step 1 _____ In your first sentence, tell the name of the person and how that person was important.

Step 2 _____ In your next sentence, write where the person was born.

Step 3 _____ In the next sentence, tell about the person's job.

Step 4 _____ In the next three or four sentences, tell a short story about the person. The story should show why the person is important.

Step 5 _____ Try to use the word *but* in one of the sentences in Step 4. Remember to use a comma!

Step 6 _____ Use a negative verb in one of the sentences in Step 4.

Step 7 _____ In the last sentence, write why you chose this person.

Step 8 _____ Use at least three of the vocabulary words or phrases presented in Activity 16, Activity 17, and Activity 18. Underline these words and phrases in your paragraph.

✔ Checklist

1. ☐ Make sure every sentence has a subject and a verb.

2. ☐ Make sure the verbs are the correct form of the simple past tense.

3. ☐ Make sure every sentence begins with a capital letter.

4. ☐ Make sure that all the proper nouns (names, cities, countries, etc.) are capitalized.

5. ☐ Make sure every sentence ends with the correct punctuation.

6. ☐ Create a title for your paragraph.

ACTIVITY 20 Peer Editing

Exchange papers from Activity 19 with a partner. Read your partner's writing. Then use Peer Editing Sheet 4 on page 255 to help you comment on your partner's writing. Be sure to offer positive suggestions and comments that will help your partner improve his or her writing. Consider your partner's comments as you revise your own writing.

Guided, structured activities help students to quickly master writing tasks.

Individual and peer **editing** opportunities in every unit provide focused guidelines for effective editing practice.

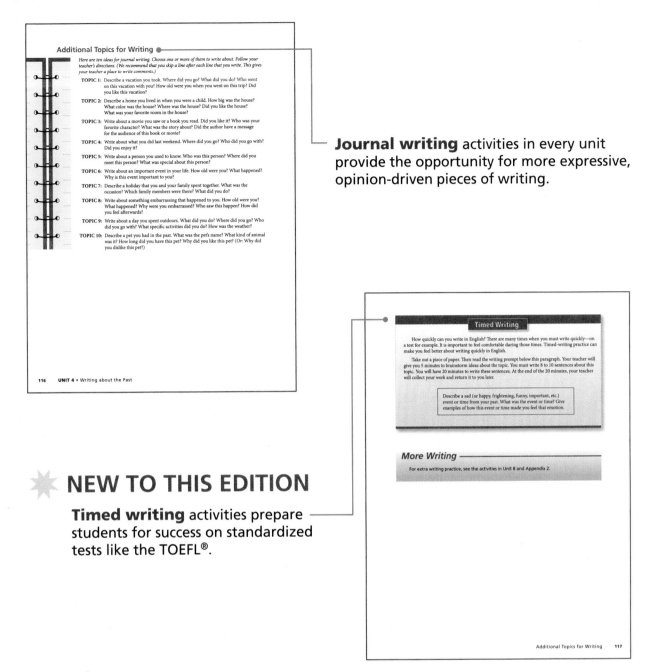

Additional Topics for Writing

Here are ten ideas for journal writing. Choose one or more of them to write about. Follow your teacher's directions. (We recommend that you skip a line after each line that you write. This gives your teacher a place to write comments.)

TOPIC 1: Describe a vacation you took. Where did you go? What did you do? Who went on this vacation with you? How old were you when you went on this trip? Did you like this vacation?

TOPIC 2: Describe a home you lived in when you were a child. How big was the house? What color was the house? Where was the house? Did you like the house? What was your favorite room in the house?

TOPIC 3: Write about a movie you saw or a book you read. Did you like it? Who was your favorite character? What was the story about? Did the author have a message for the audience of this book or movie?

TOPIC 4: Write about what you did last weekend. Where did you go? Who did you go with? Did you enjoy it?

TOPIC 5: Write about a person you used to know. Who was this person? Where did you meet this person? What was special about this person?

TOPIC 6: Write about an important event in your life. How old were you? What happened? Why is this event important to you?

TOPIC 7: Describe a holiday that you and your family spent together. What was the occasion? Which family members were there? What did you do?

TOPIC 8: Write about something embarrassing that happened to you. How old were you? What happened? Why were you embarrassed? Who saw this happen? How did you feel afterwards?

TOPIC 9: Write about a day you spent outdoors. What did you do? Where did you go? Who did you go with? What specific activities did you do? How was the weather?

TOPIC 10: Describe a pet you had in the past. What was the pet's name? What kind of animal was it? How long did you have this pet? Why did you like this pet? (Or: Why did you dislike this pet?)

116   **UNIT 4** • Writing about the Past

Journal writing activities in every unit provide the opportunity for more expressive, opinion-driven pieces of writing.

Timed Writing

How quickly can you write in English? There are many times when you must write quickly—on a test for example. It is important to feel comfortable during those times. Timed-writing practice can make you feel better about writing quickly in English.

Take out a piece of paper. Then read the writing prompt below this paragraph. Your teacher will give you 5 minutes to brainstorm ideas about the topic. You must write 8 to 10 sentences about this topic. You will have 20 minutes to write these sentences. At the end of the 20 minutes, your teacher will collect your work and return it to you later.

> Describe a sad (or happy, frightening, funny, important, etc.) event or time from your past. What was the event or time? Give examples of how this event or time made you feel that emotion.

More Writing

For extra writing practice, see the activities in Unit 8 and Appendix 2.

Additional Topics for Writing   117

NEW TO THIS EDITION

Timed writing activities prepare students for success on standardized tests like the TOEFL®.

Supplements

NEW TO THIS EDITION

The **Assessment CD-ROM with** *ExamView*® allows teachers to create tests and quizzes easily.

NEW TO THIS EDITION

The **Classroom Presentation Tool** makes instruction clearer and learning simpler.

For **Instructor's Resources** like lesson-planning tips, please visit elt.heinle.com/greatwriting.

Understanding Sentence Basics

Unit 1

GOAL: To learn how to write a correct simple sentence

*Grammar and Sentence Structure: Subjects, verbs, and objects; the verb *be*

*Sentence Development: Simple sentences

What Is a Sentence?

A **sentence** is a group of words that expresses a complete thought. The words in a sentence are in a special order. Examples of sentences are *Joe likes basketball.* and *The weather is cold today.*

Do You Know?

The sentences on the left are English. The sentences on the right are not English. Do you know what languages they are? Try to guess the languages and then check your answers on the bottom of page 35.

The class has twelve students.	Ci sono dodici studenti nella classe.
The student is from Canada.	這位學生是來自加拿大。
Mike speaks French and English.	Miklós beszél franciául és angolul.
A cat has a tail and four legs.	Pisica are o coadă și patru picioare.

Words, sentences, paragraphs, and essays are all related. Words can go together to make sentences. Sentences can go together to make a paragraph. Finally, paragraphs can be combined into an essay. In this book, you will study sentences. Then you will study sentences in paragraphs.

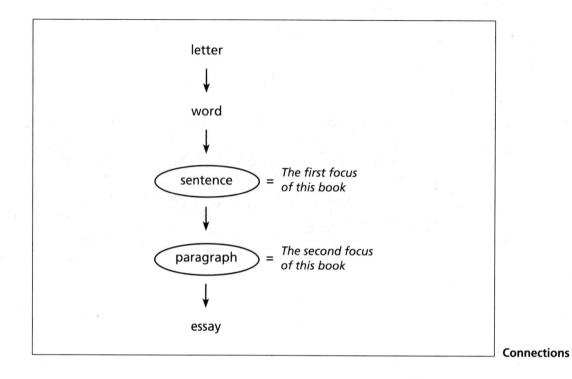

letter

↓

word

↓

sentence = *The first focus of this book*

↓

paragraph = *The second focus of this book*

↓

essay

Connections

ACTIVITY 1 Words into Sentences

Unscramble the words below to make correct English sentences. The first one has been done for you.

Topic: My family

1. is not / very big / My family /.   <u>My family is not very big.</u>

2. only four people / There are /.   _____

3. I / two parents / have /.   _____

4. José / My father's name / is /.   _____

5. My mother's name / Karina / is /.   _____

6. have / I / one brother /.   _____

7. His name / Andy / is /.   _____

8. very much / I / my family / love /.   _____

Write five to eight sentences about your family. Follow the examples in Activity 1.

Topic: My family

1. _____

2. _____

3. _____

4. _____

5. _____

6. _____

7. _____

8. _____

Working with Sentences

In this section, you will learn the basics of how to write simple sentences, including capitalization and some punctuation rules.

Writer's Note

Beginning a Sentence with a Capital Letter

In English, there are two kinds of letters: capital letters (*H, R*) and lowercase letters (*h, r*). Most of the time we use lowercase letters. However, we always begin a sentence with a **capital letter**.

Incorrect: the boxes on the table are heavy.

Correct: The boxes on the table are heavy.

Incorrect: where do you live?

Correct: Where do you live?

Look back at any five sentences in the unit so far. Can you find any sentences that do not begin with a capital letter? (The answer is "no"!)

(NOTE: See the Brief Writer's Handbook, pages 217–218, for capitalization rules.)

In English, there are three ways to end a sentence:

- with a period (.)

- with a question mark (?)

- with an exclamation point (!)

✎ Writer's Note

Ending a Sentence with a Period

The most common or usual way to end a sentence is with a **period**. A sentence that tells us information is called a statement. We usually put a period at the end of a sentence that is a statement. For example, this sentence has a period at the end. Can you find any sentences in this unit that do not end with a period? (The answer is "yes"!)

Incorrect:	Brazil is a large country
Correct:	Brazil is a large country.
Incorrect:	I do not like coffee with sugar
Correct:	I do not like coffee with sugar.

ACTIVITY 3 Unscrambling and Writing Sentences

Unscramble the groups of words on the next page to write simple sentences. Be sure to begin each sentence with a capital letter. In addition, be sure to put a period at the end of each sentence.

Topic: Something good to eat

1. spaghetti / most kids / like

    _____

2. enjoy / they / the taste of spaghetti

    _____

3. the smell of spaghetti / they / love

    _____

4. tomato sauce / on their spaghetti / some kids / put

    _____

5. like / on their spaghetti / cheese / other kids

    _____

6. is very / most kids / popular with / spaghetti

    _____

 For more practice with scrambled sentences, try Unit 1, Activity 1 on the *Great Writing 1* Web site: elt.heinle.com/greatwriting

ACTIVITY 4 Writing Simple Sentences

Copy the sentences you unscrambled in Activity 3. In each sentence, change the word spaghetti *to* ice cream. *Make other appropriate changes as necessary.*

1. _____
2. _____
3. _____
4. _____
5. _____
6. _____

Read the eight sentences below about a taxi driver. In each sentence, correct the capitalization mistake and add a period at the end. Then write the sentences on another piece of paper. The first one has been done for you.

Topic: A person and his or her job

1. M̶y̶ cousin Albert has an interesting job.

2. albert is a taxi driver

3. he is a good taxi driver

4. albert works for a large taxi company

5. the name of the taxi company is Lightning Taxi Service

6. albert drives a taxi six days a week

7. he meets fascinating people from many different places

8. albert really loves his work

Using Capital Letters

Proper Nouns

In English, the name of a specific person, place, or thing always begins with a capital letter. These types of words are called **proper nouns**. *Nelson Mandela* is the name of a specific person. *San Francisco* is the name of a specific place. *Mona Lisa* is the name of a specific thing. Can you think of more examples?

Incorrect:	My friend john works in chicago.
Correct:	My friend **J**ohn works in **C**hicago. (*a specific person, a specific place*)
Incorrect:	lucille and robby learned about world war I.
Correct:	**L**ucille and **R**obby learned about **W**orld **W**ar I. (*specific people, a specific thing*)

Common Nouns

Common nouns do not begin with a capital letter. They begin with a lowercase letter. Some examples of common nouns are *car, computer, garage, snow,* and *television.*

More Capital Letters

In English, many other kinds of words begin with capital letters. Here are some examples.

Days of the week

Incorrect:	My birthday is on monday.
Correct:	My birthday is on **M**onday.

Months

Incorrect:	The shortest month of the year is february.
Correct:	The shortest month of the year is **F**ebruary.

Languages

Incorrect:	Sireesha speaks hindi.
Correct:	Sireesha speaks **H**indi.

Countries

Incorrect:	My father is from thailand.
Correct:	My father is from **T**hailand.

(NOTE: See the Brief Writer's Handbook, pages 217–218, for capitalization rules.)

Question Marks

Geography

In English, some sentences end with a **question mark** (?). *Do you understand this? Do you have any questions?* These are examples of questions. They have a question mark at the end.

Incorrect: *Is Brazil a large country.*

Correct: *Is Brazil a large country?*

Incorrect: *Where do you live.*

Correct: *Where do you live?*

ACTIVITY 6 Geography Quiz

How well do you know geography? Unscramble the words below to write questions about geography. Then write the answers in complete sentences. Make sure the words are in the correct order. Be careful to use capital letters and end punctuation. The first one has been done for you.

1. what / the capital / of brazil / is

   Question: What is the capital of Brazil?

   Answer: The capital of Brazil is Brasilia.

2. is / what city / the white house in

   Question: _____

   Answer: _____

3. what country / the nile river in / is

   Question: _____

   Answer: _____

4. what city / is / the eiffel tower in

   Question: _____

   Answer: _____

5. what / the biggest city / in mexico / is

Question: _____

Answer: _____

6. where / are / the andes mountains

Question: _____

Answer: _____

7. is / what / the capital of saudi arabia

Question: _____

Answer: _____

8. what / the biggest province / is / in canada

Question: _____

Answer: _____

For more practice with punctuation and capitalization, try Unit 1, Activity 2 and Activity 3 on the *Great Writing 1* Web site: elt.heinle.com/greatwriting

Writer's Note

Prepositions of Place—*At*, *On*, and *In*

Three important **prepositions** are *at, on,* and *in.* These prepositions have many meanings, but one important function is to indicate location.

At is used with specific locations such as

• business names	I work at First Union Bank.
• street names with a house or business number	I live at 915 W. Norcross Street.

On is used with

• street names (without the house or business number)	I live on W. Norcross Street.

In is used with

• town or city names	I live in Houston.
• state names	I live in Texas.
• larger region names	I live in the Middle East. I live in the South.
• country names	I live in Korea. I live in the U.S.

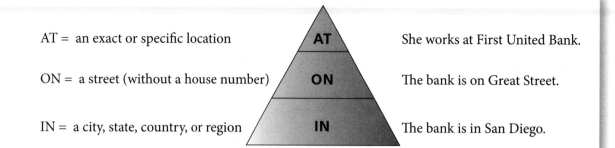

AT = an exact or specific location **AT** She works at First United Bank.

ON = a street (without a house number) **ON** The bank is on Great Street.

IN = a city, state, country, or region **IN** The bank is in San Diego.

Why do we use the pyramid to explain the uses of *at, in,* and *on*? The pyramid design is especially good to show the difference in meaning for *at, on,* and *in* for place. The top of the pyramid is a point. It is a very small, specific place. We use *at* for a specific place. We use *on* for the next largest place. Finally, we use *in* for the largest places. Look at the examples to the right of the pyramid. We use *at* for the bank, which is a specific place. We use *on* for the street, which is a larger place. We use *in* for the city, which is an even larger place.

(NOTE: For a review of common time prepositions, see the Brief Writer's Handbook, pages 225–226.)

ACTIVITY 7 Choosing the Correct Preposition

Read this paragraph about banks in a small town. Underline the correct prepositions.

EXAMPLE PARAGRAPH 1

Banks in a Small Town

It is surprising that Nelson has seven banks. Nelson is a small town (**1.** at, in, on) California. There are only about 36,000 people (**2.** at, in, on) this town. However, there are three banks, and each bank has at least two branches. The banks are National, First California, and Trust. National Bank has branches (**3.** at, in, on) 60 Green Street and (**4.** at, in, on) Hanks Avenue. First California Bank has branches (**5.** at, in, on) Princeton Street and (**6.** at, in, on) Lee Road. Trust Bank has branches (**7.** at, in, on) 27 Temple Street, (**8.** at, in, on) Whispering Street, and (**9.** at, in, on) 445 Orange Avenue. No one understands why there are seven banks (**10.** at, in, on) a small town like Nelson, California.

For more practice with prepositions of place, try Unit 1, Activity 4 on the *Great Writing 1* Web site: elt.heinle.com/greatwriting

Writer's Note

Exclamation Points

You use an **exclamation point** (!) to show emphasis or emotion about something. Exclamation points are not used often, but when a sentence expresses surprise or strong emotion, it is appropriate to use an exclamation point.

Simple Fact:	It is snowing.
With Surprise:	It is snowing!
Simple Fact:	I won the lottery last night.
With Surprise:	I won the lottery last night!

ACTIVITY 8 Statement, Question, or Exclamation?

Read each sentence. If it is a statement, write S on the line and put a period (.) at the end of the sentence. If it is a question, write Q on the line and put a question mark (?) at the end of the sentence. If it is an exclamation, write E on the line and put an exclamation point (!) at the end of the sentence. The first two have been done for you.

1. __Q__ How many days are in a month?

2. __S__ The answer depends on the month.

3. _____ Only four months have thirty days

4. _____ An example of a month with only thirty days is September

5. _____ Other months have thirty-one days

6. _____ Examples of months with thirty-one days are July and December

7. _____ Which month never has thirty days

8. _____ The answer is February

9. _____ February usually has only twenty-eight days

10. _____ Everyone in my family was born in February

○	FEBRUARY					○
Sun	Mon	Tue	Wed	Thu	Fri	Sat
						1
2	3	4	5	6	7	8
9	10	11	12	13	14	15
16	17	18	19	20	21	22
23	24	25	26	27	28	

Rewrite the questions on the lines. Be sure to use capital letters and question marks correctly. Then ask a classmate the questions. Write your classmate's answers. Use capital letters and periods.

1. what is your name

   Question: _____

   Answer: _____

2. where are you from

   Question: _____

   Answer: _____

3. where do you live

   Question: _____

   Answer: _____

4. how many people are in your family

   Question: _____

   Answer: _____

5. do you have a car

   Question: _____

   Answer: _____

6. what food do you like to eat

   Question: _____

   Answer: _____

7. what is your favorite place to visit

   Question: _____

   Answer: _____

8. what is your favorite movie

   Question: _____

   Answer: _____

Here are some sentences and questions about Costa Rica. The words and phrases in each sentence are scrambled. First, put the sentence or question parts in the correct order. Then add capital letters. Finally, add a period, a question mark, or an exclamation point at the end of each sentence.

Topic: A country

1. costa rica / where / is

   _____

2. in central america / a small country / costa rica / is

   _____

3. between panama / and nicaragua / it / is

   _____

4. this country / is / between the pacific ocean / and the caribbean sea

   _____

5. approximately four million / is / the population / of costa rica

   _____

6. many tourists / there / go

   _____

7. wild animals / they / see / in the jungle

   _____

8. in the world / the most beautiful country / it is

   _____

9. want to visit / I / this beautiful country

   _____

10. costa rica / do you want / to visit

   _____

Answer the following questions and write eight to ten sentences about the country that you choose. Use capital letters, periods, question marks, and exclamation points correctly.

Topic: A country

1. What country do you want to visit? _____

2. Why do you want to visit this country? _____

   _____

   _____

3. Where is this country located? _____

   _____

4. How big is this country? _____

   _____

5. What is the capital of this country? _____

   _____

6. What is one famous monument or important place in this country? _____

   _____

7. Briefly describe this monument or place. _____

   _____

   _____

8. What do you know about food in this country? _____

   _____

   _____

The Parts of a Sentence

Every English sentence must have a subject and a verb.

Sentence Development

The Simple Sentence

The basic sentence pattern that you are studying in this unit is called a **simple sentence**. A simple sentence has one subject-verb combination. Sometimes there is a noun or pronoun object and/or other information after the verb.

Simple Sentence: S + V + O

	Subject	+	Verb	+	Object	+	Other Information
a.	Maria Simms		plays		the piano		well.
b.	She		practices		the piano		every day.
c.	Maria		likes		classical piano music		a lot.
d.	She		enjoys		listening		to German music.

Simple Sentence: S + V

	Subject	+	Verb	+	Object	+	Other Information
e.	Maria Simms		plays				extremely well.
f.	She		practices				for three hours.
g.	Maria		goes				to piano class every day.

- Some verbs, such as *like* and *enjoy,* must have an object after them. (These are called transitive verbs. In a dictionary, these verbs are marked with the letters *v.t.*)

    Incorrect: Maria likes a lot.

    Correct: Maria likes <u>classical piano music</u> a lot.

- Some verbs, such as *go* and *arrive*, can never have an object after them. (These verbs are called intransitive verbs. In a dictionary, these are marked with the letters *v.i.*)

    Incorrect: Maria goes piano class.

    Correct: Maria <u>enjoys</u> piano class.

    Correct: Maria <u>goes to</u> piano class.

- Some verbs, such as *play* and *practice*, can have an object or not have an object. (In a dictionary, these verbs are marked with only the letter *v.*)

Grammar and Sentence Structure

Subjects, Verbs, and Objects

In English, every sentence has two main parts: the subject and the verb. As you study the following simple sentences, look for this pattern.

Subject

The **subject** is the person or thing that does the action. The subject comes before the verb. Look at these simple sentences. The subjects are underlined.

Maria Simms plays the piano.

She practices the piano every day.

Maria likes classical piano music a lot.

Maria goes to piano class every week. (no object)

Verb

The **verb** is usually the action word in the sentence. The verb comes after the subject. Examples of verbs are *go, speak, write, swim,* and *watch.* Some verbs do not have much action. Examples are *be* (*am, is, are, was, were*), *like, want,* and *need.* Look at these simple sentences. The verbs are circled.

Maria Simms (plays) the piano.

She (practices) the piano every day.

Maria (likes) classical piano music a lot.

Maria (goes) to piano class every week. (no object)

Object

The **object** is the thing or person after the verb. The object answers the questions *Who?* or *What?* The object is the thing or person that receives the action of the verb. Look at these simple sentences. The objects are in boxes. (These objects are also called direct objects.)

Maria Simms plays $\boxed{\text{the piano}}$.

She practices $\boxed{\text{the piano}}$ every day.

Maria likes $\boxed{\text{classical piano music}}$ a lot.

Maria goes to piano class every week. (no object)

Fragments: Checking for the Subject and the Verb

Every sentence should have a subject and a verb. It is easy for student writers to leave out the subject or the verb. A sentence without a subject or without a verb is called a **fragment**. A fragment is a piece of a sentence.

Incorrect: John is my brother. Works at Ames Bank in Miami. (no subject)

Correct: <u>John</u> (is) my brother. <u>He</u> (works) at Ames Bank in Miami.

Incorrect: Many Japanese people a white car. (no verb)

Correct: <u>Many Japanese people</u> (have) a white car.

Correct: <u>Many Japanese people</u> (drive) a white car.

In writing, a fragment is a serious mistake. A fragment shows the reader that the writer did not check his or her work carefully. When you write your sentences, check each of them to make sure that there is a subject AND a verb.

Commands

In **command** (imperative) sentences, the subject is *you*. However, the word *you* is not usually stated.

Examples: Open the door now! (NOT: *You* open the door now!)

Do not say that word! (NOT: *You* do not say that word!)

ACTIVITY 12 Subjects and Verbs

Read these sentences about making tuna salad. Underline each subject and circle each verb. The first one has been done for you.

1. <u>Tuna salad</u> (is) easy to make.

2. The ingredients are simple and cheap.

3. Two ingredients are tuna fish and mayonnaise.

4. I also use onions, salt, and pepper.

5. First, I cut up the onion.

6. Then I add the tuna fish and the mayonnaise.

7. Finally, I add some salt and a lot of pepper.

8. Without a doubt, tuna salad is my favorite food!

 For more practice with the parts of a sentence, try Unit 1, Activity 5 and Activity 6 on the *Great Writing 1* Web site: elt.heinle.com/greatwriting

ACTIVITY 13 Sentence or Fragment?

Read each group of words. If it is a fragment, write F on the line. If it is a complete sentence, write S on the line. If it is a question, write Q. The first two have been done for you.

1. ___S___ Billy Mitchell lives in a big apartment.

2. ___F___ My mother breakfast every morning.

3. _____ Is incredibly delicious.

4. _____ Does Carol have a car?

5. _____ They my cousins from Miami.

6. _____ You a student.

7. _____ Michael likes classical music.

8. _____ Nancy and Jeanine very best friends.

9. _____ The girls play soccer after school.

10. _____ I am from Colombia.

 For more practice with sentence fragments, try Unit 1, Activity 7 on the *Great Writing 1* Web site: elt.heinle.com/greatwriting

Grammar and Sentence Structure

The Verb *Be*

The most frequently used verb in the English language is the verb *be*. *Be* has five main forms: *am, is, are, was,* and *were.*

I <u>am</u> a student.

My writing <u>is</u> good.

My friends <u>are</u> here.

I <u>was</u> a good student in kindergarten.

The questions on the quiz <u>were</u> difficult.

There are four commonly used sentence patterns for the verb *be*. The information that follows the verb *be* is usually an adjective (a word that describes a noun), a noun, or a place phrase.

1.	Subject	+	*be*	+	Adjective
	This tuna salad		is		delicious.
2.	Subject	+	*be*	+	Noun
	This tuna salad		is		a delicious dish.
3.	Subject	+	*be*	+	Place phrase
	This tuna salad		is		on the table.

When you begin a sentence with *There,* the subject follows the verb *be.*

4.	*There*	+	*be*	+	Subject	+	(Extra information: usually place or time)
	There		is		a tuna salad sandwich		on the table.
	There		were		two empty plates		on the table this morning.
	There		was		a big sale on canned tuna		last week.

NOTE: More practice on writing sentences with *There is/There are* can be found on pages 73–75 in Unit 3.

When you have a sentence with *be* + verb + -*ing*, then *be* is not the main verb.

Example: I am studying English.   →   verb: *am studying* (from *study*)

but

I am a student.   →   verb: *am* (from *be*)

ACTIVITY 14 Subjects and Verbs

Read these eight sentences. Underline the subjects and circle the verbs. The first one has been done for you.

EXAMPLE PARAGRAPH 2

(1.) There (are) four <u>books</u> | on the desk | . (2.) The two large books are | textbooks | .
(3.) The grammar book is | green | . (4.) The composition book is | next to the grammar book | .
(5.) It is | blue | . (6.) The other two books are | smaller | . (7.) They are | workbooks | .
(8.) The textbooks are | easy | , but the workbooks are | difficult | .

ACTIVITY 15 Identifying Words and Phrases

Look at the sentences in Activity 14. Identify the words or phrases in boxes as an adjective, *a* noun, *or a* place phrase. *The first one has been done for you.*

1. on the desk = *a place phrase*

2. textbooks = _____

3. green = _____

4. next to the grammar book = _____

5. blue = _____

6. smaller = _____

7. workbooks = _____

8. easy = _____

9. difficult = _____

Read these sets of three sentences. Complete the sentences with the correct form of be.

1. There _____ seven colors in a rainbow. These colors _____ red, orange, yellow, green, blue, indigo, and violet. My favorite rainbow color _____ green.

2. There _____ twenty-six letters in the English alphabet. Twenty-one of these letters _____ consonants. The other five letters _____ vowels.

3. There _____ different students in my class. Five students _____ from Venezuela. Only one student _____ from China.

4. There _____ an insect on the window. It _____ a caterpillar. It _____ light yellow, and it has spots on it.

5. There _____ a huge map of the world on the wall in our classroom. The water areas _____ light blue. The land areas _____ various colors.

✎ Writer's Note

Using Supporting Ideas with *There is/There are* Sentences

Sometimes a simple paragraph begins with a *There is/There are* sentence. This sentence tells the reader that something exists. A good paragraph also contains sentences that are related to the topic or idea in the first sentence.

EXAMPLE PARAGRAPH 3

There is a huge map of the world on the wall in our classroom. The water areas are light blue. All of the oceans, seas, and lakes are light blue. The land areas are various colors. The countries are red, yellow, green, blue, and tan. Heavy black dots are the capital cities. This map is so big that students in the back of the room can see all of the country names.

1. The first sentence begins with *There is.* It tells the reader about a map.

2. The second sentence describes a part of the map. (water areas)

3. The third sentence describes a part of the map. (examples of water areas)

4. The fourth sentence describes a part of the map. (land areas)

5. The fifth sentence describes a part of the map. (examples of land areas)

6. The sixth sentence describes a part of the map. (capital cities)

7. The last sentence talks about how big the map is and how all the students can see it.

ACTIVITY 17 Writing Paragraph Beginnings

In numbers 1–3, write two additional sentences that are related to the first sentence. In numbers 4–6, write a sentence that begins with there is *or* there are. *Then add two related sentences. Follow the examples from Activity 16.*

1. There are _____* people in my family. _____

   _____

   _____

   _____

2. There are _____* students in my English class. _____

   _____

   _____

   _____

3. There are many unique animals in a zoo. _____

   _____

   _____

   _____

4. _____

   _____

   _____

   _____

5. _____

   _____

   _____

   _____

6. _____

   _____

   _____

   _____

*Add the correct number.

Read the simple sentences in this paragraph. Identify the underlined words as a subject (S), verb (V), or adjective (ADJ). The first one has been done for you.

Making Hummus

S

<u>Hummus</u> is a very easy snack to make. The ingredients are <u>simple</u> and <u>cheap</u>. <u>Two ingredients</u> are chickpeas and crushed garlic. <u>I</u> also use lemon juice and olive oil. First, I <u>wash</u> and <u>mash</u> the chickpeas. Then I <u>add</u> the crushed garlic. Finally, I <u>mix in</u> the lemon juice and olive oil. Some people add tahini paste. This fast snack is now ready to eat. <u>It</u> is my favorite snack.

Sentences in Paragraphs

You can put sentences together to make a paragraph. All the sentences in a paragraph are about the same topic.

Writer's Note

Sentences and Paragraphs

A group of words that tell about one idea is called a **sentence**. A group of sentences that tell about one topic or one idea is called a **paragraph**.

Look at the sentences in Activity 12 and Activity 18 again. How are they different? In Activity 12, the sentences are in a list. In Activity 18, the sentences are not in a list. They are in a special format. This format is called a paragraph. What do you know about paragraphs? You will study much more about paragraphs beginning in Unit 2.

Use these subjects and verbs to make correct subject-verb combinations and write them on the lines below. Remember that the subject usually comes before the verb in sentences. You will use some words more than once. Some blanks can have more than one answer.

Caroline	she	her lunch break	Anderson Supermarket		
wakes up	starts	attends	likes	enjoys	works	is

EXAMPLE PARAGRAPH 5

A Great Place to Work

(**1.**) _____ at Anderson Supermarket. (**2.**) _____

there on Monday, Tuesday, and Thursday. She does not work there on Wednesday because

(**3.**) _____ classes at Jefferson Community College. On her workdays,

(**4.**) _____ at 6 A.M. (**5.**) _____ her workday

at 8 A.M. (**6.**) _____ from 8 A.M. to 5 P.M. (**7.**) _____

is from 12:30 to 1:30. (**8.**) _____ her job very much. (**9.**) _____

_____ her coworkers, too. For Caroline, (**10.**) _____

_____ a great place to work.

For more practice with the word order of subjects and verbs, try Unit 1, Activity 8 on the *Great Writing 1* Web site: elt.heinle.com/greatwriting

✎ Writer's Note

The Title of a Paragraph

What is the title of this textbook? Look on the front cover. Write the title here.

_____

What is the title of Example Paragraph 1 on page 10? Write the title here.

_____

A **title** gives you information about what is in a book, a song, a movie, or a paragraph. Here are some rules to follow when you write a title for your paragraphs.

1. A good title is usually very short. Sometimes it is only one word. *Frankenstein, Cinderella,* and *Titanic* are all titles. Can you think of other one-word titles?

2. A good title is usually not a complete sentence. *Jobs for the Future, A World Traveler,* and *An Old Family Photo* are all titles of paragraphs in this book. These titles are not complete sentences. Can you think of some titles of books you have read?

3. A good title catches the reader's interest. It tells the reader about the main topic, but it does not tell about everything in the paragraph. *A Long Flight, An Important Invention,* and *My First Car* are all titles of paragraphs in this book. Each one gives you a good idea of what the paragraph will be about. However, it does not give you all the information. You must read the paragraph to find out more.

4. A good title also follows special capitalization rules. The first letter of the first word is always capitalized. Only capitalize the first letter of the important words in the title. Do not capitalize a preposition or an article unless it is the first word.

5. A good title does not have a period at the end.

ACTIVITY 20 Working with Titles

Each of these titles breaks one of the rules listed on pages 24–25. Rewrite each one correctly. Be prepared to share your answers with your classmates and explain which rule(s) the incorrect title breaks.

1. Today Was the Best day of My Life

   _____

2. THE COMBUSTION ENGINE

   _____

3. A Handbook For International Students In Canada

   _____

4. The Early Search for Gold in California.

   _____

5. My Paragraph

   _____

6. How to Make a Phone Call to Another Country Without Spending a Lot of Money

   _____

ACTIVITY 21 Editing Simple Sentences

Read the sentences about world geography. Some of the sentences are fragments (missing subject or missing verb) or have errors with punctuation or capitalization. If the sentence is correct, write C on the line. If the sentence contains an error, write X on the line and tell what the error is. Then write the correct sentence below. The first two have been done for you.

1. X (fragment—verb missing) _____ Mexico not near Great Britain.

   Mexico is not near Great Britain. _____

2. X (capitalization) _____ The Statue of Liberty is in new york.

   The Statue of Liberty is in New York. _____

3. _____ Burundi is in africa.

   _____

   _____

4. _____ Canada bigger than the United States.

   _____

   _____

5. _____ A popular city in Florida is Miami?

   _____

   _____

6. _____ Nepal is north of India.

   _____

   _____

7. _____ Visits the Mayan ruins in Central America every year!

   _____

   _____

8. _____ Bolivia no seaports.

_____

_____

9. _____ Three main groups of people live in Malaysia.

_____

_____

10. _____ Austria and Hungary in Europe.

_____

_____

11. _____ Is between Mexico and Canada.

_____

_____

12. _____ Of Thailand is about 65,000,000.

_____

_____

ACTIVITY 22 Editing: Grammar and Sentence Review

Read the following paragraph. There are 10 mistakes: 5 missing be verbs, 2 missing subjects, 2 capitalization mistakes, and 1 punctuation mistake. Find and correct the mistakes. The first one has been done for you.

The Beauty of Tuscany

Tuscany ^is^ a beautiful region in Italy. Is famous for cities such as florence, Siena, and Pisa. The appenine Hills in Tuscany? Tuscany also famous for the production of beautiful ceramics. For example, bowls, vases, and oil jars very popular with tourists. Tuscany has so many interesting places to see. Assisi and Siena two beautiful cities that many people love to visit. Is a wonderful place to visit!

⚒ Building Better Sentences

Correct and varied sentence structure is essential to the quality of your writing. For further practice with the sentences and paragraphs in this unit, go to Practice 1 on pages 233–234 in Appendix 1.

Building Better Vocabulary

ACTIVITY 23 Word Associations

Circle the word or phrase that is most closely related to the word or phrase on the left. If necessary, use a dictionary to check the meaning of words you do not know. The first one has been done for you.

1. surprise	known	(unknown)
2. to work	at the beach	at the office
3. to understand	to add	to know
4. ingredients	when you read	when you cook
5. simple	complicated	not difficult
6. cheap	low price	high price
7. finally	the last	the first
8. to cut up	make into many pieces	keep in one piece
9. an addition	something put in	something taken out
10. to attend	to do something	to be present
11. a break	a short rest	a short process
12. to enjoy	to dislike	to like
13. to meet	a new person	a new product
14. a region	a size	a place
15. famous	well-known	professional

ACTIVITY 24 Using Collocations

Fill in each blank with the word on the left that most naturally completes the phrase on the right. If necessary, use a dictionary to check the meaning of words you do not know. The first one has been done for you.

1. popular / tasty — a _____popular_____ actor
2. to / from — add lemon juice _____ the hummus
3. a supermarket / a concert — attend _____

4. region / branch   a bank _____

5. result / break   a surprising _____

6. break / movie   an interesting _____

7. simple / cheap   _____ answer

8. a chair / a sentence   understand _____

9. mayonnaise / an onion   cut up _____

10. meet / add   _____ ingredients

ACTIVITY 25 Parts of Speech

Study the following word forms. In the sentences on the right, choose the best word and write it in the blank space. Be sure to use the right form of the verbs. If necessary, use a dictionary to check the meaning of words you do not know. The first one has been done for you. (NOTE: The word in bold is the original word that appears in the unit.)

Noun	Verb	Adjective	Sentence Practice
addition	**add**	Ø	1. She _____ adds _____ sugar to her coffee.
			2. We plan to build an _____ to our home.
attendance	**attend**	Ø	3. The teacher checks the students' _____ every day.
			4. Do you want to _____ the concert tomorrow?
popularity	Ø	**popular**	5. Britney is a _____ singer.
			6. The _____ of motorcycles is incredible!
happiness	Ø	**happy**	7. She is very _____ because it is her birthday.
			8. The key to _____ is not easy.
work	**work**	Ø	9. My sisters _____ in a supermarket.
			10. Do you enjoy your _____?

Noun endings: -tion, -ance, -ity, -ness

Original Student Writing

Choose ONE of the three practices below. For the practice you choose:

1. *Read the first question.*

2. *Fill in the answer. This will be the topic.*

3. *Then answer the questions about the topic. Be sure to use complete sentences with a subject and a verb.*

4. *Use at least three of the vocabulary words or phrases presented in Activity 23, Activity 24, and Activity 25. Underline these words and phrases in your sentences.*

5. *After you write your sentences, check the spelling and grammar.*

Practice 1

Question 1a: What is your favorite food?

Answer 1a: My favorite food is _____

Question 1b: What country does this food come from?

Answer 1b: _____

_____

Question 1c: What ingredients are in this food?

Answer 1c: _____

_____

Question 1d: How do you prepare this food?

Answer 1d: _____

_____

Question 1e: Why do you like this food?

Answer 1e: _____

_____

Practice 2

Question 2a: What food do you like to cook?

Answer 2a: I like to cook _____

Question 2b: What ingredients do you need?

Answer 2b: _____

_____

Question 2c: What is the first thing you do?

Answer 2c: _____

_____

Question 2d: What do you do next?

Answer 2d: _____

_____

Question 2e: How long does it take to prepare this food?

Answer 2e: _____

_____

Practice 3

Question 3a: Who is the most interesting person in your family?

Answer 3a: The most interesting person in my family is _____

Question 3b: Why is this person interesting?

Answer 3b: _____

_____

Question 3c: How old is this person?

Answer 3c: _____

_____

Question 3d: What does this person look like?

Answer 3d: _____

_____

Question 3e: Why do you like this person?

Answer 3e: _____

_____

Editing

Good writers need editors to help them make their writing correct. For your writing in this book, you and your classmates (peers) are your editors.

✏ Writer's Note

Self-Editing

An editor is someone who makes sure the writing is correct. A good editor checks the grammar and punctuation. A good editor also makes sure the writing is clear and easy to understand. There should be two editors when you write a paragraph for class: you and a classmate. First, you will read your own work for mistakes. Then a classmate (a peer) will read your work and help you find ways to make it better.

✏ Writer's Note

Peer Editing for the Writer

A peer is someone who is equal to you. Your peers are the other students in your class.

It is important to hear what other people think about your writing. You need to know if they can understand your ideas. A good way to make sure that your writing is clear is to let someone else read your paper and make suggestions about it. This is called **peer editing**.

This is what usually happens in peer editing:

1. Another person reads your writing.

2. That person gives you suggestions and ideas for making your writing better.

3. You listen carefully to what your peer says.

4. You may want to make the changes your peer suggests. If the comments are negative, remember that the comments are about the writing, not about you!

✏ Writer's Note

Peer Editing for the Reader

When you read your classmate's paper, be polite. Choose your words carefully. Do not say, "This is bad grammar," or "What is this?" It is better to say, "You forgot to put the word *at*," or "What does this sentence mean?"

Say things the way you would want someone to tell you!

ACTIVITY 27 Peer Editing

Exchange books with a partner and look at Activity 26. Read your partner's writing. Then use Peer Editing Sheet 1 on page 249 to help you comment on your partner's writing. Be sure to offer positive suggestions and comments that will help your partner improve his or her writing. Consider your partner's comments as you revise your own writing.

Journal Writing

Many good writers write in a journal for practice and for ideas.

✎ Writer's Note

Journal Writing—Write, Write, Write!

How can you become a better writer? The activities in this book will help you. The most important thing, however, is to write as much and as often as you can.

The Benefit of Practice

Think about people who play tennis well. These people were excited about tennis. Perhaps they read books about tennis. They probably went to see a professional tennis match. These activities alone cannot make people become good tennis players. They have to <u>practice</u>. It does not matter if at first they hit the ball the wrong way. The most important thing is to hit the ball again and again. This is how people get better at tennis.

In some ways, you are like the tennis player. You want to be a good writer. Reading this book and doing the activities are helpful. Reading books and articles will help you, too. One of the best ways to become a good writer in English is to write as much as possible and as often as possible.

Practice in a Journal

An excellent way to practice is to write in a **journal.** A journal is a notebook in which you write things regularly. You practice expressing yourself in written English.

In a journal, you choose a specific topic and write about it. You try to express your ideas about the topic so that readers can understand what you mean. Journal topics can be general or specific. Here are some topics for journal writing:

General Topics: sports, swimming, food, books, travel, fashion, music

Specific Topics: my favorite sport, why I am a vegetarian, my first airplane trip

Teacher Response

Your teacher will read your journal from time to time. Your teacher will not mark all of the grammar mistakes. A journal uses informal language. It is like a conversation between the writer and the reader (teacher). If you write about a city, do not take information from a book. Instead, write about why you want to visit that city or about the first time you visited it.

Your teacher may write some comments in your journal. Your teacher might make one or two comments about the language, especially if you repeat the same mistake.

If you have any questions, you can ask your teacher in your journal. For example, if you want to know if you used a grammar point or a vocabulary word correctly, you can write a question in your journal.

Sample Journal

March 21

Sometimes I feel lonely here. My parents are far away, but my brother is here. His name is Nelson. He is two years older than I am. He wants to study business administration. He looks like my father. He is 22 years old.

Before we came here, Nelson and I went to New York City. We visited some cousins there. Hotels in New York (expensive). We stayed with our cousins. That saved us a lot of money.

I do not my cousins very often, so I was happy. Sometimes I feel bad because I do not know them very well.

student writing

This is interesting information. I didn't know that your brother is at this school, too. Do you live together? I've been to New York City, too, and I know that hotels are VERY expensive there.

Grammar: I circled two places where you forgot to put a verb. Can you think of some verbs for those sentences?

It was easy to understand the message of your writing here. Keep up the good work!

teacher comments

Additional Topics for Writing

Here are ten ideas for journal writing. Choose one or more of them to write about. Follow your teacher's directions. (We recommend that you skip a line after each line that you write. This gives your teacher a place to write comments.)

TOPIC 1: Write about your favorite pet. Why do you like this animal? Do you have one at home? What does the animal look like? What is its name? How old is it?

TOPIC 2: Write about your favorite type of weather. Why do you like this weather? What kind of activities do you do in this weather?

TOPIC 3: Write about your mother or your father. Include his/her name, age, and occupation.
What kind of personality does your mother or father have?

TOPIC 4: Write about a toy you remember from your childhood. What kind of toy was it? How long did you have it? Who gave it to you? Do you still have it? If not, what happened to it?

TOPIC 5: Write about your experience learning English. Why are you studying English? How do you feel about English? What is easy for you to understand in English? What are some difficulties you have in English?

TOPIC 6: Write about your favorite type of fashion in clothing. What kind is it? Why do you like it?

TOPIC 7: Write about an "extreme" sport, such as bungee jumping. How do you feel about this sport? Do you want to try this sport? Why or why not? Describe the types of people who enjoy these kinds of sports.

TOPIC 8: What are some things you love about your country? Why are those things important to you?

TOPIC 9: Write about your home. How many rooms are in your home? What color is it? How old is it? Do you like it? What is your favorite room?

TOPIC 10: Write about what you do in your leisure (free) time. Who do you spend the time with? What activities do you do? How long do you spend doing these activities? Are your free-time activities the same during the week and on weekends?

More Writing

For extra writing practice, see the activities in Unit 8 and Appendix 2.

Answers to questions on page 1: Italian, Japanese, Hungarian, and Romanian.

Connecting Sentences and Paragraphs

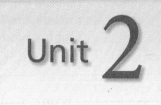

Unit 2

GOAL: To learn about paragraph structure

*Grammar and Sentence Structure: Adjectives; subject pronouns; possessive adjectives

Sentences: Using Adjectives

You already know that a sentence must have a subject and a verb. (Remember from Unit 1 that a sentence without a subject or without a verb is called a fragment and is a serious mistake in English writing.) However, you can make a sentence much more interesting if you add descriptive words. These descriptive words are called adjectives. They describe nouns.

Grammar and Sentence Structure

Word Order: Adjectives before Nouns

Nouns are the names of people, places, things, or ideas. Examples are *teacher, doctor, student, city, park, book,* and *pencil.*

Adjectives are words that describe nouns. Examples are *good* teacher, *busy* doctor, *new* student, *crowded* city, *green* park, *heavy* book, and *yellow* pencil.

A simple way to combine two short sentences when there is an adjective is to put the adjective before the noun. Look at the following examples.

Two Short Sentences	Better Writing

I have a <u>book</u>. It is <u>heavy</u>.
      NOUN   ADJ.
	I have a <u>heavy</u> <u>book</u>.
	        ADJ. NOUN

This is my <u>car</u>. It is <u>new</u>.
         NOUN   ADJ.
	This is my <u>new</u> <u>car</u>.
	         ADJ. NOUN

Mr. Vicks is a <u>teacher</u>. He is <u>excellent</u>.
          NOUN   ADJ.
	Mr. Vicks is an <u>excellent</u> <u>teacher</u>.
	          ADJ. NOUN

Rachel draws <u>small</u> <u>pictures</u>. She draws <u>ink</u> <u>pictures</u>.
       ADJ.   NOUN   ADJ. NOUN
	Rachel draws <u>small</u> <u>ink</u> <u>pictures</u>.
	          ADJ. ADJ. NOUN

Be careful! Make sure you put the adjective before the noun, not after.

Incorrect: I have a **car red** with a **top black**.

Correct: I have a red car with a black top.

Incorrect: We ate **salad green** with **potatoes fried**.

Correct: We ate green salad with fried potatoes.

Be careful! Adjectives do not have a plural form to describe plural nouns.

Incorrect: There are **rares** books in the library.

Correct: There are rare books in the library.

Incorrect: Do you like **populars** songs?

Correct: Do you like popular songs?

(NOTE: See the Brief Writer's Handbook, pages 228–229, for more information about order of adjectives.)

ACTIVITY 1 Editing: Nouns and Adjectives

Combine the following sentences. You will have to eliminate a few words. Remember to use a capital letter at the beginning and a period at the end of each new sentence. The first one has been done for you.

1. Robert owns a car. The car is red.

   Robert owns a red car.

2. I do not like this weather. The weather is humid.

   _____

3. Paris is a city in France. This city is beautiful.

   _____

4. Ali has a job. The job is part-time.

   _____

5. They like to drink cola. The cola is diet.

   _____

6. Niloofar reads folk tales. They are international.

   _____

7. My mother grows roses. The roses are big. The roses are beautiful.

   _____

8. Juan works for a company. The company is small. The company is independent.

   _____

9. My grandparents live in a town. It is a farming town. The town is small.

_____

10. Sharon rents a house on Smith Street. The house is tiny. The house is white.

_____

 For more practice with using adjectives, try Unit 2, Activity 1 on the *Great Writing 1* Web site: elt.heinle.com/greatwriting

Grammar and Sentence Structure

Word Order: Adjectives after the Verb *Be*

You have learned that adjectives come before the noun they describe.

The <u>young</u> <u>boy</u> carried the <u>heavy</u> <u>box</u>.
   ADJ. NOUN   ADJ. NOUN

In this sentence, *young* describes *boy* and *heavy* describes *box*.

Complements

Adjectives can be used in another way. If the main verb of a sentence is a form of *be*, the adjective can come *after* the verb. The adjective is called a **complement**.

The <u>boy</u> is <u>young</u>.   The <u>box</u> is <u>heavy</u>.
NOUN   ADJ.   NOUN   ADJ.

My <u>uncle</u> is <u>rich</u>.   <u>Paris</u> is <u>beautiful</u>.
NOUN   ADJ.   NOUN   ADJ.

That <u>music</u> is <u>loud</u>! <u>Jim</u> is <u>sleepy</u>.
NOUN   ADJ.   NOUN   ADJ.

That <u>house</u> is <u>big</u>.   That <u>house</u> is <u>green</u>.   That <u>house</u> is <u>big</u> and <u>green</u>.
NOUN   ADJ.   NOUN   ADJ.   NOUN   ADJ.   ADJ.

Adjectives are very important in writing, so make sure you use them correctly.

Read the following paragraph. There are 10 adjectives in the paragraph. Underline them. If you need help finding the adjectives, look at the numbers in parentheses on the left side of the paragraph. These numbers tell you how many adjectives are in each line. The first one has been done for you.

EXAMPLE PARAGRAPH 7

My Ideal Vacation

(2)   I have a dream to visit Alaska. The weather is <u>beautiful</u> there. I love cold weather. When

(1)   the temperature is low, I have energy! I also want to visit Alaska because I love nature.

(3)   Alaska is **pure** and natural. I dream about its **scenic** landscape. In addition, there are

(1)   wild animals. Finally, I want to

(1)   learn important information about

(1)   the **native** people of Alaska. I hope

(1)   to visit this wonderful state soon.

pure: clean; not polluted
scenic: having a beautiful natural landscape
native: born in a certain place; originated

For more practice with adjectives after the verb *be*, try Unit 2, Activity 2 on the *Great Writing 1* Web site: elt.heinle.com/greatwriting

What Is a Paragraph?

In Unit 1, you studied sentences. A **sentence** is a group of words that expresses a complete thought. You learned that a sentence has two main parts: the subject and the verb. The words in a sentence are in a special order.

Most people write more than one sentence at a time. Sometimes they write a paragraph. A **paragraph** is a group of sentences. All of the sentences in a paragraph are about one specific topic.

> A paragraph has three main parts: the topic sentence, the body, and a concluding sentence.

The **topic sentence** is one sentence that tells the main idea of the whole paragraph. This sentence is usually the first sentence of the paragraph.

The **body** of a paragraph has sentences with information that supports the topic sentence. It is important to remember that *every* sentence in the body must be connected in some way to the topic sentence.

In addition to the topic sentence and the body, paragraphs generally have a third part: a **concluding sentence**. The concluding sentence is at the end of the paragraph. It is a brief summary of the information in the paragraph. Some paragraphs, especially short paragraphs, do not have a concluding sentence.

Working with the Whole Paragraph

Let's see how the parts of a paragraph work together to make a good paragraph that is easy to read.

✎ Writer's Note

Topic Sentences

Every good paragraph has a topic sentence. If there is no topic sentence, the reader may be confused because the ideas will not be organized clearly. When you write a paragraph, remember to use a topic sentence. It gives the general topic of the whole paragraph.

ACTIVITY 3 Paragraph Study

Read the following two paragraphs. Answer the questions that follow.

EXAMPLE PARAGRAPH 8

My Favorite Color

It is obvious that my favorite color is blue. I have six blue shirts. I wear blue jeans almost every day. I have three pairs of light blue tennis shoes. I own a blue car, and my computer is blue. Other colors are nice, but I like blue the best.

1. How many sentences are in this paragraph? _____

2. What is the main topic of this paragraph? (*Circle the letter of the answer.*)

   a. The writer likes blue computers.　 b. The writer likes blue.　 c. The writer likes light blue clothes.

3. What is the topic sentence? Remember that the topic sentence tells the main idea of the whole paragraph. Write it here.

   _____

4. The writer gives five examples of blue things. What five blue things does the writer have? Write five sentences about these blue things. The first one has been done for you.

   a. The writer has six blue shirts._____

   b. _____

   c. _____

   d. _____

   e. _____

5. Sometimes paragraphs have a concluding sentence. A concluding sentence is a summary of the ideas in the paragraph. If there is a concluding sentence, write it here.

_____

6. Read the paragraph again. Can you find at least two descriptive adjectives? Write them below.

_____

Taipei 101

I work in one of the world's tallest buildings—Taipei 101. This building is in Taipei's business **district**. Taipei 101 opened to the public in 2004. It is made of **steel** and glass panels, so it has a beautiful silver color. It has one hundred and one **floors**. There are even five more levels below the building! Many international businesses have offices in Taipei 101. There are great places to shop in the building, too. I am **proud** to work in such an important place.

a district: an area
steel: a very strong metal

a floor: a level of a building
proud: a very happy feeling of satisfaction

1. How many sentences are in this paragraph? _____

2. What is the main topic of this paragraph? (*Circle the letter of the answer.*)

   a. information about a city

   b. information about a person

   c. information about a building

3. What is the topic sentence? Write it here.

_____

_____

4. Answer these questions in complete sentences.

   a. Where is the building?

   _____

   b. How old is the building?

   _____

   c. What color is the building?

   _____

   d. How many floors does the building have?

   _____

5. Sometimes paragraphs have a concluding sentence. A concluding sentence is a summary of the ideas in the paragraph. If there is a concluding sentence, write it here.

   _____

   _____

6. Read the paragraph again. Can you find at least four descriptive adjectives? Write them below.

   _____

Writer's Note

Indenting the First Line of Every Paragraph

Look at the first line of Example Paragraph 8 on page 40. How is the formatting different from the other lines in the paragraph?

Look at the first line of Example Paragraph 9 on page 41. Do you see how the first line is also moved in? This space is called an indentation. The action of making this space at the beginning of a paragraph is to **indent**.

It is important to indent the first line of every paragraph. Always remember to indent!

For more practice with the parts of a paragraph, try Unit 2, Activity 3 and Activity 4 on the *Great Writing 1* Web site: elt.heinle.com/greatwriting

ACTIVITY 4 Copying a Paragraph

On the lines below, copy the six sentences about spaghetti from Activity 3, Unit 1, pages 4–5. Be sure to indent the first line. Use correct punctuation at the end of each sentence. Give this paragraph a title. When you finish, read your new paragraph. Underline the topic sentence.

EXAMPLE PARAGRAPH 10

_____

_____

_____

_____

_____

_____

_____

_____

_____

_____

_____

_____

_____

Answer the questions. Be sure to use complete sentences. When you finish, write your sentences in paragraph form on the lines provided below.

1. Who is your favorite singer? My favorite singer is _____

2. What country does he/she come from? _____
   _____

3. What kind of music does he/she sing? _____
   _____

4. What is your favorite song by this singer? _____
   _____

5. Why do you like this singer? _____
   _____

Now write your sentences in paragraph form. Be sure to give your paragraph a title.

EXAMPLE PARAGRAPH 11

_____

_____

_____

_____

_____

_____

_____

_____

_____

Working with Topic Sentences

Every paragraph must have a good topic sentence. The topic sentence gives the main idea of the paragraph. The topic sentence should not be too specific or too general. The topic sentence tells the reader what the paragraph is about.

ACTIVITY 6 Topic Sentences

Read each paragraph and the three topic sentences below it. Then choose the best topic sentence and write it on the line. Read the paragraph again. Make sure that the topic sentence gives the main idea for the whole paragraph. Remember to indent!

Beautiful Snow?

_____

_____ Snow is beautiful when it falls. After a few days, the snow is not beautiful anymore. It starts to **melt**, and the clean streets become **messy**. It is difficult to walk anywhere. The **sidewalks** are **slippery**. Snow also causes traffic problems. Some roads are closed. Other roads are **hard** to drive on safely. Drivers have more **accidents** on snowy roads. I understand why some people like snow, but I do not like it very much.

melt: to change from ice to liquid
messy: sloppy; dirty
sidewalk: paved walkway on the side of roads

slippery: causing a person to slip or slide, usually because of a smooth surface
hard: difficult
an accident: a car crash

   a. In December, it usually snows.

   b. Some people like snow, but I do not.

   c. I love snow.

Maria and Her Great Job

_____

_____ She works at Papa Joe's Restaurant. She serves about sixty people every day.

Maria can remember all the dinner orders. If there is a problem with any of the food, she takes it

back to the kitchen immediately. Maria wants every customer to have a good meal at the restaurant.

    a. My cousin Maria is an excellent server.

    b. My cousin Maria works at Papa Joe's Restaurant.

    c. Maria's customers do not eat big meals.

My Favorite City

_____

_____ I love to see all the interesting things there. The city is big, exciting, and full of

life. I always visit the Empire State Building and the Statue of Liberty. I also visit Chinatown. At night,

I go to **shows** on Broadway. The food in the city is excellent, too. I truly enjoy New York City.

a show: a live performance on stage

    a. I like to see the Empire State Building and the Statue of Liberty.

    b. New York is a very big city.

    c. My favorite city in the world is New York City.

Read each paragraph and the four topic sentences below it. Then choose the best topic sentence and write it on the line. Read the paragraph again. Make sure that the topic sentence gives the main idea for the whole paragraph. Be sure to indent!

EXAMPLE PARAGRAPH 15

Pasta, Pasta, Pasta

_____

_____ Pasta tastes great. Sometimes I eat it **plain**. I also like it with butter or **Parmesan** cheese. Another reason I like pasta is the **variety**. Pasta includes spaghetti, macaroni, vermicelli, ravioli, lasagna, and many other kinds. In addition, pasta is very easy to prepare. I can make pasta in less than ten minutes. Finally, pasta is a very healthy food for me. A plate of pasta has about 300 **calories**, but it has only three grams of fat. I love to eat pasta every day!

plain: with nothing added; simple   **variety:** many different kinds
Parmesan: a hard, dry Italian cheese   **calories:** measurement of heat energy of food

   a. Everybody loves pasta.

   b. Spaghetti and macaroni are kinds of pasta.

   c. Pasta is my favorite food.

   d. Pasta comes from Italy.

Good Teachers

_____

_____ First of all, good teachers are **patient**. They never **rush** their students. Good teachers explain things without getting **bored**. In addition, they are organized. They plan what happens in every class. Good teachers are also **encouraging**. They help students understand the subject. Finally, good teachers are **fair**. They treat all students the same. These are some of the most important qualities of good teachers.

patient: calm; untiring   **encouraging:** helpful; comforting
rush: to go very quickly   **fair:** equal; impartial
bored: not interested

   a. All good teachers are patient.
   b. Good teachers have special qualities.
   c. I like my teachers.
   d. Some teachers are good, but some teachers are not so good.

A Radio Station for Everyone

_____ Radio Station 97.5 FM plays Spanish music. For people who like rock music, there is Station 98.1. The music on Radio Station 101.5 is all jazz. Station 103.6 plays blues music during the day and jazz at night. Station 103.9 plays many different kinds of music. Young people listen to Station 105.7 for dance music. Our city is certainly lucky to have so many kinds of music stations.

a. This city offers radio stations for everyone.

b. This city does not have many Spanish music stations.

c. I do not like rock music very much.

d. I like jazz a lot.

Grammar and Sentence Structure

Subject Pronouns

A pronoun is a word that takes the place of a noun. A **subject pronoun** comes before the verb, just like any subject usually does. In English, there are seven subject pronouns.

Singular	Plural
I	we
you	you
he/she/it	they

Examples with sentences:

Singular	Plural
I live in Panama.	**We** live in Panama.
You are from Africa.	**You** are from Africa.
He works in a factory.	**They** work in a factory.

Read the following paragraph. Replace the nouns in parentheses with a subject pronoun. The first one has been done for you.

Two Doctors

Rosemarie Bertrand and Michael Scott are interesting people. Rosemarie is a doctor in Scotland. (**1.** Rosemarie Bertrand) _____She_____ is married to Michael. (**2.** Michael Scott) _____ is also a doctor. (**3.** Rosemarie and Michael) _____ live in Edinburgh. (**4.** Edinburgh) _____ is a historic city. Dr. Bertrand and Dr. Scott have an office together downtown. (**5.** The office) _____ is busy every day. (**6.** Rosemarie and Michael) _____ work hard five days a week. On weekends, however, (**7.** Rosemarie and Michael) _____ like to travel to the countryside. (**8.** The countryside) _____ is a beautiful and relaxing escape from all their hard work.

 For more practice with subject pronouns, try Unit 2, Activity 5 on the *Great Writing 1* Web site: elt.heinle.com/greatwriting

Writer's Note

Writing about People: Proper Nouns and Subject Pronouns

When you write about a person, you use that person's name. The name is called a **proper noun**. (For more information about proper nouns, see page 7.) Study these examples:

<u>George Woods</u> teaches at Briar Elementary School. <u>He</u> teaches math and science there.
    NOUN   PRONOUN

<u>Alisa</u> lives in the city. <u>She</u> likes the noise and the crowds.
NOUN   PRONOUN

It is correct to use a person's name when you write one or two sentences, but in a paragraph or in conversation, good writers and speakers do not use the person's name many times. Instead, they use a subject pronoun (*I, you, he, she, it, we,* or *they*).

REMEMBER: Do not repeat the proper noun many times. Replace it with a pronoun.

Working with the Body of the Paragraph

Earlier in this unit, you practiced topic sentences. Every topic sentence must have supporting sentences—these sentences make up the body of the paragraph. This body of supporting sentences is directly related to the topic sentence. Supporting sentences give information about the topic sentence. Therefore, the supporting sentences are just as important as the topic sentence.

One mistake that many writers make is writing sentences that are not related to the topic sentence. Plan what your supporting information will be so that it is related to the topic sentence.

Writer's Note

Supporting Sentences: The Body of a Paragraph

You have learned that a paragraph has three main parts: the topic sentence, the body, and the concluding sentence. Remember, the body consists of sentences that give supporting information and ideas about the topic sentence. Therefore, it is important for *every* sentence to be related to the topic sentence.

Make sure that each sentence provides **support**, **details**, or **examples** for the ideas in the topic sentence. Cut out any unrelated or unconnected ideas!

ACTIVITY 9 The Body of the Paragraph

Read each paragraph carefully. Underline the topic sentence. In each paragraph, one supporting sentence does not belong because it is not directly connected to the topic sentence. It does not fit the ideas in the paragraph. Put parentheses ( ) around the one sentence that does not belong.

EXAMPLE PARAGRAPH 19

Keeping Score in American Football

Keeping score in American football is more difficult than keeping score in soccer. In soccer, each goal is **worth** one point. For example, if a team scores five goals in a game, then the team's score is five points. In American football, the scoring system is different. When a player carries the ball across the end zone, he scores a touchdown. A touchdown is worth six points. When a player kicks the football between the goal posts, that team gets one point or three points. Another sport that has easy scoring is basketball.

keeping score: maintaining a count of the total points in a game
worth: equal to; valued at

Making Chili

Chili is an easy dish to prepare. Fried chicken is also easy to prepare. To make chili, cut up two large onions. Then fry them in a little vegetable oil. You can add fresh garlic and some **diced** chili peppers. When the onions are soft, add two pounds of **ground** beef. **Stir** the onions and beef until they are **fully** cooked. Sprinkle one tablespoon of red chili powder on top. Next, add four cups of diced tomatoes, two cups of water, and one can of red beans. Finally, add salt and pepper. Cover the saucepan and cook over low heat for about one hour. If you follow this simple **recipe**, you will have a delicious **meal**!

chili: a thick stew made with meat, beans, and tomatoes
diced: cut into little squares
ground: broken into small pieces
stir: to mix

fully: completely; entirely
a recipe: directions for cooking food
a meal: breakfast, lunch, or dinner

Celsius and Fahrenheit Temperatures

Changing temperatures from Celsius to Fahrenheit is not difficult. First, **multiply** the Celsius temperature by 9. Then **divide** this answer by 5. When you finish, add 32 **degrees** to your answer. The result is the temperature in Fahrenheit. Many countries report temperatures in Celsius, but the United States uses Fahrenheit. For example, if the Celsius temperature is 20, you multiply 20 by 9. Then you divide the answer, 180, by 5. The result is 36. Next, add 32, and you have the correct Fahrenheit temperature. Now you know how to change a temperature from Celsius to Fahrenheit.

multiply: $2 \times 2 = 4$
divide: $15 \div 3 = 5$
degrees: units of measurement for temperature: $98° = 98$ degrees

Grammar and Sentence Structure

Possessive Adjectives

When you want to talk about something that belongs to someone or something, you use a **possessive adjective**. A possessive adjective shows possession. It answers questions related to ownership such as *Whose house? Whose books?* and *Whose television?*

In English, there are seven possessive adjectives: *my, your, his, her, its, our,* and *their.* A possessive adjective always occurs with a noun.

my	I live in <u>my</u> father's house.
your	Do you have <u>your</u> books?
his	He lives with <u>his</u> father.
her	She does not carry money in <u>her</u> purse.
its	A butterfly moves <u>its</u> wings quickly.
our	We write all <u>our</u> papers on a computer.
their	They can bring <u>their</u> CDs.

(NOTE: See the Brief Writer's Handbook, page 224, for more information about possessive adjectives.)

Read the following paragraph. Write the missing possessive adjectives. The first one has been done for you.

EXAMPLE PARAGRAPH 22

Caroline and Her Sisters

Caroline has two sisters and one brother. (**1.**) _____Their_____ names are Ashley, Margaret, and Nick. Ashley and Margaret live with (**2.**) _____ parents. They are high school students. Ashley likes to play sports. (**3.**) _____ favorite sport is softball. She is a very good player. Margaret does not like sports, but she loves music. She plays (**4.**) _____ guitar every afternoon after school. Ashley and Margaret have the same friends. (**5.**) _____ friends go to the same school. (**6.**) _____ brother, Nick, is in college. (**7.**) _____ major is business administration. Caroline's brother and sisters are all very different, but she loves (**8.**) _____ **siblings** very much.

a sibling: a brother or a sister

This paragraph contains many subject pronouns and possessive adjectives. Underline the correct forms in parentheses ( ). The first one has been done for you.

EXAMPLE PARAGRAPH 23

(I, <u>My</u>) Grandmother

A very important person in (**1.** I, my) life is (**2.** I, my) grandmother. (**3.** She, Her) name is Evelyn Anna Kratz. (**4.** She, Her) life is very interesting. (**5.** She, Her) is 89 years old. (**6.** She, Her) comes from Poland. (**7.** She, Her) can speak English well, but (**8.** she, her) first language is Polish. My grandmother comes from a large family. (**9.** She, Her) has two brothers. (**10.** They, Their) names are Peter and John. (**11.** I, My) grandmother has two sisters, too. (**12.** They, Their) names are Karina and Maria. (**13.** I, My) like to listen to (**14.** my, her) grandmother's stories because (**15.** they, their) are so interesting. In (**16.** I, my) opinion, they are the most interesting stories in the world.

For more practice with subject pronouns and possessive adjectives, try Unit 2, Activity 6 on the *Great Writing 1* Web site: elt.heinle.com/greatwriting

Read the topic sentence and body of each paragraph carefully. In each paragraph, there are two sentences that do not belong. Put parentheses ( ) around these two sentences.

The *New* States

Four U.S. states begin with the word *new*. New Hampshire, New Jersey, and New York are in the Northeast, but New Mexico is in the Southwest. Arizona is also in the Southwest. New Hampshire is a small state with about one million people. New Jersey is also a small state, but its population is about eight million people. The most **well-known** of the *new* states is New York. The population of New York is about twenty million. New Mexico is the largest of these four states, but its population is small. There are no states that begin with the word *old*. Although all these states begin with *new*, they are all very different.

well-known: popular, familiar, famous

An Incredible Neighbor

My neighbor Mrs. Wills is an **amazing** person. She is 96 years old. My grandmother lived to be 87. Mrs. Wills lives alone, and she takes care of herself. In the morning, she works in her beautiful garden. She also does all of her own cooking. She does not like to cook rice. She cleans her own house. She even puts her heavy garbage can by the street for trash collection. She pulls the can slowly to the **curb**, and she goes up and down the steps to her door by herself. I hope to have that much energy and ability when I am 96 years old.

amazing: remarkable; wonderful; incredible   **the curb:** the side of the street

My Office

My office is a comfortable place to work. On the left side of the room, there is a big **wooden** desk. My computer sits on top of the desk, and the printer sits under the desk. I keep paper **files** in the drawers. On the right side of the room, there are two beautiful bookcases. My father makes bookcases and other wood furniture. These bookcases are full of books, magazines, and computer software. There is also a telephone and a fax machine in my office. I have trouble remembering my fax number. There is a closet next to the fax machine. All my office supplies are there. I enjoy my office very much.

wooden: made of wood   **files:** documents; papers

Writer's Note

Checking for the Verb

Do you sometimes forget to include the verb in a sentence? Many writers make this mistake. This is the rule: Every sentence needs a verb.

Incorrect:	My father's name Samuel.
Correct:	My father's name **is** Samuel.
Incorrect:	Many people in Switzerland French.
Correct:	Many people in Switzerland **speak** French.
Incorrect:	Some elementary schools computers for the students.
Correct:	Some elementary schools **have** computers for the students.

When you check your writing, look at each sentence carefully. Is there a verb? Remember that every sentence needs a verb.

Read the following sentences. Five sentences are missing the verb be. *Find these five sentences and then add the correct form of the* be *verb. The first one is done for you. Now put the sentences in order to form a proper paragraph. Write their number order on the line to the left of each sentence. The first one is done for you.*

Staying Healthy

_____ a. Doctors say that one hour of **moderate** exercise each day can keep you in good shape.

_____ b. First, think about the food you eat.

___1___ c. It is easy to stay healthy if you **follow** some simple **steps**.

_____ d. Take time to **appreciate** the good things in life.

_____ e. You can follow these steps to help yourself stay healthy.

_____ f. The best **types** of food fruits and vegetables.

_____ g. In addition, exercise good for the body and the mind.

_____ h. Finally, relaxation very important.

_____ i. It important to eat a lot of them every day.

_____ j. Next, **consider** some exercise.

moderate: an average amount   **steps:** directions   **a type:** a kind
follow: to obey, do   **appreciate:** to enjoy   **consider:** to think about

 For more practice with checking for the verb, try Unit 2, Activity 7 on the *Great Writing 1* Web site: elt.heinle.com/greatwriting

Working with Concluding Sentences

You learned about topic sentences and supporting sentences. All good paragraphs have a topic sentence. The topic sentence is usually (but not always) the first sentence in a paragraph. The body of a paragraph contains several supporting sentences. These sentences must relate to the topic sentence.

A paragraph may end with another part called the concluding sentence. The concluding sentence often gives a summary of the information in the paragraph. In many cases, the information in the topic sentence is similar to the information in the concluding sentence. However, it could also be a suggestion, opinion, or prediction.

Look at the topic sentences and concluding sentences from these paragraphs in this unit.

	Paragraph 7, Page 39	**Paragraph 8, Page 40**	**Paragraph 9, Page 41**
Topic Sentence	I have a dream to visit Alaska.	It is obvious that my favorite color is blue.	I work in one of the world's tallest buildings—Taipei 101.
Concluding Sentence	I hope to visit this wonderful state soon.	Other colors are nice, but I like blue the best.	I am proud to work in such an important place.

ACTIVITY 14 Concluding Sentences

Copy the topic sentence and the concluding sentence from each paragraph indicated. How are the two sentences the same? How are they different? Discuss your answers with a partner.

1. Example Paragraph 12, page 45

   Topic sentence: _____

   Concluding sentence: _____

2. Example Paragraph 13, page 46

   Topic sentence: _____

   Concluding sentence: _____

3. Example Paragraph 14, page 46

   Topic sentence: _____

   Concluding sentence: _____

4. Example Paragraph 15, page 47

   Topic sentence: _____

   Concluding sentence: _____

5. Example Paragraph 16, page 48

   Topic sentence: _____

   Concluding sentence: _____

6. Example Paragraph 17, page 49

   Topic sentence: _____

   Concluding sentence: _____

Read each paragraph. Then read the concluding sentences below it. Circle the letter of the best concluding sentence.

Monday

I hate Monday for many reasons. One reason is work. I get up early to go to work on Monday. After a weekend of fun and relaxation, I do not like to go to work. Another reason that I do not like Monday is that I have three meetings every Monday. These meetings last a long time, and they are **extremely** boring. Traffic is also a big problem on Monday. There are more cars on the road on Monday. Drivers are in a bad **mood**, and I must be more careful than usual.

extremely: very
mood: disposition; humor

a. Monday is worse than Tuesday, but it is better than Sunday.
b. I do not like meetings on Monday.
c. These are just a few reasons why I do not like Monday.

Good Luck, Bad Luck

Superstitions usually relate to luck. Some of the luck is good. For example, some people believe that the number seven is lucky. Other people think that if you see a shooting star, you can make a wish and it will come true. However, most superstitions talk about bad luck. **For instance**, many people believe that it is bad luck to open an umbrella inside a house. They also think that it is bad luck if a black cat walks in front of you. Other people think that if your left ear is burning, someone is saying something bad about you.

for instance: for example

a. People believe exactly the same superstitions.
b. It is amazing how many good and bad superstitions there are!
c. The worst superstition is about breaking a mirror.

Buying a Car

Buying a car **requires** careful planning. Do you want a new or a used car? This depends on how much money you can spend. Sometimes a used car needs repairs. What style of car do you want? You can look at many different models to help you decide. Next, do you want extra **features** in your new car? Adding lots of extra features makes a car more expensive. Finally, you have to decide where you will buy your car.

require: to need
features: options, such as air-conditioning or tinted windows

    a. It is important to think about all these things when you are buying a car.
    b. The most important thing is the kind of car that you want to buy.
    c. Will you buy your new car from a friend or a car dealer?

ACTIVITY 16 Editing: Grammar and Sentence Review

Read this paragraph. There are seven mistakes: three mistakes with adjectives, two missing be *verbs, and two capitalization mistakes. Find and correct the mistakes.*

Aspirin

aspirin is an incredible type of medicine. This small white pill is not a drug new. We do not know exactly why or how it works. However, millions of people use aspirin every day. we take aspirin for reasons many. Aspirin good for headaches, colds, and pain. Aspirin can help with so many different health problems. Aspirin is a medicine simple, but it great.

Building Better Sentences

Correct and varied sentence structure is essential to the quality of your writing. For further practice with the sentences and paragraphs in this unit, go to Practice 2 on page 234 in Appendix 1.

Building Better Vocabulary

ACTIVITY 17 Word Associations

Circle the word or phrase that is most closely related to the word or phrase on the left. If necessary, use a dictionary to check the meaning of words you do not know.

1. an opinion	a fact	a belief
2. a headache	pain	relaxation
3. to consider	to talk to	to think about
4. to spend	money goes out	money comes in
5. to wear	a hat	a tire
6. furniture	sofa	rug
7. to come from	origin	destination
8. afternoon	daylight	darkness
9. to serve	to give	to take
10. traffic	vehicles	pedestrians
11. downtown	city center	suburb
12. to prepare	food	a headache
13. to organize	to make neat	to make messy
14. a variety	many choices	few choices

ACTIVITY 18 Using Collocations

Fill in each blank with the word on the left that most naturally completes the phrase on the right. If necessary, use a dictionary to check the meaning of words you do not know.

1. idea / ideal	_____ job	
2. of / for	a variety _____ ideas	

3. do / follow	_____ a recipe
4. to / for	to prepare _____ an emergency
5. take / ride	_____ a taxi
6. be / get	_____ worth
7. in / on	to major _____ engineering
8. in / on	to be _____ the third floor
9. eat / take	_____ an aspirin
10. high / tall	_____ temperature

ACTIVITY 19 Parts of Speech

Study the following word forms. For the sentences on the right, choose the best word and write it in the blank space. Be sure to use the correct form of the verb. If necessary, use a dictionary to check the meaning of words you do not know. (NOTE: The word in bold is the original word that appears in the unit.)

Noun	Verb	Adjective	Sentence Practice
dream	**dream**	Ø	1. She _____ about becoming a famous singer.
			2. My _____ is to travel to India.
love	**love**	love_ly_	3. Your dress is _____.
			4. Mario and Yumiko _____ hip-hop music.
problem	Ø	problem_atic_	5. There is a _____ with my car's air-conditioning.
			6. The economic situation is _____.
enjoy_ment_	**enjoy**	enjoy_able_	7. The live music is here for everyone's _____.
			8. We always have an _____ time on vacation.
pat_ien_ce	Ø	**patient**	9. Good teachers have a lot of _____.
			10. My mother is a very _____ woman.

Noun endings: -ment, -ence

Adjective endings: -ly, -atic, -able

Original Student Writing

Answer the following questions and write eight to ten sentences about travel. Put a check (✓) next to each question as you answer it. Use at least three of the vocabulary words or phrases presented in Activity 17, Activity 18, and Activity 19 in your sentences. Underline these words and phrases in your paragraph. Copy your sentences into a paragraph below. Then use the checklist that follows to edit your work.

Topic: Travel

☐ 1. What city do you want to visit? _____

☐ 2. What kind of transportation do you need to get to this city? _____

☐ 3. What are some reasons to go there? Think of at least three reasons. (Use adjectives in your descriptions.)

   a. Reason 1: _____

   b. Reason 2: _____

   c. Reason 3: _____

☐ 4. List two or three special activities that you can do in this city.

   a. Activity 1: _____

   b. Activity 2: _____

   c. Activity 3 (optional): _____

☐ 5. How long do you want to stay in this city? _____

☐ 6. Are you looking forward to visiting this city? (Answer in a complete sentence.) _____

_____

_____

✔ Checklist

1. ☐ Use adjectives to describe this city.

2. ☐ Indent the first line of your paragraph.

3. ☐ Check the first sentence (topic sentence) and the last sentence (concluding sentence). Are they similar in meaning?

4. ☐ Check each sentence in your paragraph. Is every sentence related to your topic?

_____

_____

_____

_____

_____

_____

_____

_____

_____

_____

_____

ACTIVITY 21 Peer Editing

Exchange books with a partner and look at Activity 20. Read your partner's writing. Then use Peer Editing Sheet 2 on page 251 to help you comment on your partner's writing. Be sure to offer positive suggestions and comments that will help your partner improve his or her writing. Consider your partner's comments as you revise your own writing.

Additional Topics for Writing

Here are ten ideas for journal writing. Choose one or more of them to write about. Follow your teacher's directions. (We recommend that you skip a line after each line that you write. This gives your teacher a place to write comments.)

TOPIC 1: Write about New York City. What do you know about it? Do you want to visit this city? Why or why not?

TOPIC 2: Write about swimming or another sport. Do you like to practice this sport? How often? Why do you enjoy this sport?

TOPIC 3: Write about your favorite kind of music. Why do you like this music? How do you feel when you listen to this music?

TOPIC 4: Write about how to use an object such as a cell phone. Explain the steps involved in using this object.

TOPIC 5: Write about credit cards. What is your opinion about them? Are they helpful or dangerous? Do you use them?

TOPIC 6: Write about a good weekend plan. What do you like to do on weekends? Who do you spend your weekends with?

TOPIC 7: Choose a person in your class to write about. Explain how the person looks and what his or her personality is like.

TOPIC 8: Write about a famous person you like. Who is this person? What is this person's job? Why do you like this person?

TOPIC 9: Write about something that you do not like. Give three reasons why you do not like this thing.

TOPIC 10: Write about your favorite subject in school. Why do you like this subject? What kinds of things do you practice in this subject?

More Writing

For extra writing practice, see the activities in Unit 8 and Appendix 2.

Writing about the Present

GOAL: To learn how to write sentences in the simple present tense

*   **Grammar and Sentence Structure:** Simple present tense; object pronouns; *a* and *an*

*   **Sentence Development:** Simple and compound sentences

Begin with the Simple Present Tense

When you write about daily habits and activities or things that are generally true, use the **simple present tense.**

Grammar and Sentence Structure

Simple Present Tense: Statements and Questions

In English, the simple present tense can be divided into two categories: regular verbs and the verbs *be* and *have.* Do you know the following verb forms?

Simple Present Tense Verb Forms: Statements		
Verb *be*	I **am** you **are** he / she / it **is**	we **are** you (plural) **are** they **are**
Verb *have*	I **have** you **have** he / she / it **has**	we **have** you (plural) **have** they **have**
Verb *live* (regular)	I **live** you **live** he / she / it **lives**	we **live** you (plural) **live** they **live**
Verb *go* (regular)	I **go** you **go** he / she / it **goes**	we **go** you (plural) **go** they **go**

Simple Present Tense Verb Forms: Questions

Verb *be*	Am I . . . ? Are you . . . ? Is he / she / it . . . ?	Are we . . . ? Are you (plural) . . . ? Are they . . . ?
Verb *have*	Do I have . . . ? Do you have . . . ? Does he / she / it have . . . ?	Do we have . . . ? Do you (plural) have . . . ? Do they have . . . ?
Verb *live*	Do I live . . . ? Do you live . . . ? Does he / she / it live . . . ?	Do we live . . . ? Do you (plural) live . . . ? Do they live . . . ?
Verb *go*	Do I go . . . ? Do you go . . . ? Does he / she / it go . . . ?	Do we go . . . ? Do you (plural) go . . . ? Do they go . . . ?

NOTE: All verbs except *be* must add *do* or *does* to make a question.

In this unit, you will practice writing sentences and paragraphs in the simple present tense.

ACTIVITY 1 Simple Present Tense Forms

Read each sentence. Write the correct form of the verb in parentheses.

EXAMPLE PARAGRAPH 32

Uncle Charlie

My Uncle Charlie (**1.** be) _____ a wonderful man. He (**2.** be) _____

an **entrepreneur**. He began his restaurant business ten years ago. Now he enjoys great success. In

his restaurant, he (**3.** have) _____ ten waiters, two managers, and three chefs. Uncle

Charlie (**4.** work) _____ very hard in his restaurant. Sometimes he is there seven

days a week. He and his wife Valerie always (**5.** go) _____ to the restaurant at night

to make sure that the customers are happy. I (**6.** love) _____ Uncle Charlie and Aunt

Valerie, and I really appreciate all their hard work. (**7.** you / know) _____ somebody

like my uncle?

entrepreneur: a person who owns his/her own business

ACTIVITY 2 The Verb *Be* in the Simple Present Tense

Read this paragraph from Giacomo to his new classmate. Fill in the missing be *verbs.*

My Classmates

My classmates come from all over the world. José (**1.**) _____ from Spain, so he

speaks Spanish perfectly. Kuniko and Yasuhiro (**2.**) _____ Japanese, but they do

not sit next to each other in class. Yuri (**3.**) _____ from Ukraine, and he plays

soccer very well. The Al-Ahmad brothers (**4.**) _____ from Dubai, and they

(**5.**) _____ both very nice. What about me? I (**6.**) _____ from Italy,

and I love to sing in class. We (**7.**) _____ all very good friends, and I hope we can

be friends forever. Where (**8.**) _____ you from?

  For more practice with the simple present tense of *be* and *have*, try Unit 3, Activity 1 on the *Great Writing 1* Web site: elt.heinle.com/greatwriting

ACTIVITY 3 Paragraph Order

Read the following sentences. Number them in the correct paragraph order. The first two sentences have been done for you.

Jim's Daily Routine

_____ a. After this part-time job, he goes home, eats a quick dinner, studies, and does his homework.

___2___ b. He studies engineering at City College.

_____ c. He goes to school for six hours.

_____ d. Jim knows that this lifestyle is stressful.

___1___ e. Jim is a very busy student.

_____ f. Every day, he wakes up at 7:00 in the morning, takes a shower, and then rushes off to school.

_____ g. He also knows that the stress will end soon, and he will get a professional job.

_____ h. After school, he goes to the local mall where he works in a sporting goods store.

Read the sentences in Activity 3. Make the following changes and rewrite the paragraph on the lines.

1. *Change the subject of the story,* Jim, *to* Jim and Billy.

2. *You will have to make certain changes to the verb forms and to some nouns and pronouns, too.*

EXAMPLE PARAGRAPH 34

Jim and Billy's Daily Routine

Jim and Billy are very busy students.

 For more practice with changing singular to plural, try Unit 3, Activity 2 on the *Great Writing 1* Web site: elt.heinle.com/greatwriting

Writer's Note

Using Contractions

A **contraction** is a short version of two words combined, such as a pronoun and a verb (*I'm = I am*). The apostrophe (') shows where a letter has been left out. Here are some common contractions with *be*:

I am = I'm   we are = we're

you are = you're   you (plural) are = you're

he is = he's / she is = she's / it is = it's   they are = they're

Some instructors believe contractions are too informal for academic writing. Be sure to ask your instructor if using contractions is acceptable.

For practice with contractions, try Unit 3, Activity 3 on the *Great Writing 1* Web site: elt.heinle.com/greatwriting

ACTIVITY 5 Writing a Paragraph from Pictures

Study the pictures on the next page. They tell a story. Then read the incomplete paragraph. Fill in the blanks based on the pictures. Write the full sentence for the last two sentences. (NOTE: The numbers in the paragraph correspond to the pictures.)

EXAMPLE PARAGRAPH 35

One Family's Morning Routine

The Lee family is very busy on weekday mornings. (**1.**) Every morning, Susan Lee, the oldest daughter, wakes up and _____ for her parents and **siblings.** She loves to cook! (**2.**) When breakfast is ready, the rest of the family _____. The kids eat breakfast quickly. (**3.**) After they eat, Susan's father and mother _____. (**4.**) At 8:30 A.M., Mr. Lee _____. (**5.**) Then he and the kids _____ to Mrs. Lee. (**6.**) Mr. Lee and the kids _____ the **minivan** so that he can take them to school. (**7.**) _____. (**8.**) A few minutes later, _____.

a sibling: a brother or sister   **a minivan:** a large family car, usually with sliding doors

Read the following paragraph. There are 7 errors. Most of the sentences are missing either the subject or the verb. Write the corrections above the errors. The first one has been done for you.

The City of Budapest

Budapest ∧ is one of the most interesting capitals of Europe. Is a romantic city, and it has many interesting tourist places to visit. One example the Danube River. It separates Budapest into Buda and Pest. In addition, visitors traditional Hungarian food. The most popular food goulash soup. The people of Budapest friendly and helpful to tourists. When travel to Europe, you can visit Budapest and have a very good time.

✎ **Writer's Note**

Review: *There Is / There Are*

• The expressions *there is* and *there are* come at the beginning of a sentence to show that something exists in a certain place.

• Follow *there is* with a singular noun.

• Follow *there are* with a plural noun.

• You must use the word *there* in this kind of sentence.

• Writers often use *there is* and *there are* with a place phrase.

   Look at the following examples.

   Incorrect: There **is** ten people in my office.

   Correct: There are ten people in my office.

   Incorrect: **Is** a desk in the room.

   Correct: There is a desk in the room.

   Incorrect: **Are** apples on the table.

   Correct: There are apples on the table.

   Incorrect: **A** concert at the university tomorrow.

   Correct: There is a concert at the university tomorrow.

(NOTE: For an introduction to *there is* and *there are*, see page 21 in Unit 1.)

Read this paragraph about a classroom. Study the four examples of there is *and* there are *in the paragraph and answer the questions.*

A Description of My Classroom

My classroom is a very colorful room. (**1.**) *There are* twenty desks in the room. Each desk has a dark brown seat and a shiny white top. On the left side of the room, (**2.**) *there is* a world map. This map shows all the different countries in the world, and each country is a different color. On the right side of the room, (**3.**) *there are* two posters. The first poster is green. It has a list of fifty common verbs. The second poster has the names and pictures of fruits and vegetables. It is white, but the writing is black. Finally, (**4.**) *there are* some pictures of wild animals above the blackboard. These objects make my classroom colorful.

a. Is (1.) singular or plural? _____ Why? _____

b. Is (2.) singular or plural? _____ Why? _____

c. Is (3.) singular or plural? _____ Why? _____

d. Is (4.) singular or plural? _____ Why? _____

e. Is there a map in the room? _____ Where? _____

f. Is there a calendar in the room? _____ Where? _____

g. Is there a cat in the room? _____ Where? _____

h. Are there animal pictures in the room? _____ Where? _____

Look at the picture of the living room. On the lines, write ten sentences about the objects in the picture. Use there is *and* there are.

1. _____
2. _____
3. _____
4. _____
5. _____
6. _____
7. _____
8. _____
9. _____
10. _____

Read this paragraph about the English alphabet. Find the 4 mistakes. Circle the mistakes and correct them. On the lines below, explain your corrections.

The English Alphabet

There have twenty-six letters in the English alphabet. There is five vowel letters and twenty-one consonant letters. The five vowels are *a, e, i, o,* and *u.* The letters *w* and *y* is sometimes vowels, especially when they come after other vowels. Three letters have the *a* sound in them. These letters is *a, j,* and *k.* Nine letters have the *e* sound in them. These are *b, c, d, e, g, p, t, v,* and *z.* If you want to speak English well, you have to learn the twenty-six letters of the English alphabet.

1. _____

2. _____

3. _____

4. _____

ACTIVITY 10 Editing: Capitalization Review

You studied capitalization in Unit 1. Read the following paragraph about the TOEFL exam. There are 10 errors in capitalization. Can you find them all? Circle the capitalization errors and write the corrections above the circled words. The first one has been done for you.

The TOEFL

Do you know about the TOEFL®? It is the Test of English as a Foreign Language. Most
                                                        U
international students who want to study at a university in the ⓤnited states take this test. it measures english language ability. The test comes from Educational Testing Service in new jersey. It is a very long test. the TOEFL tests several subject areas, including reading, listening, speaking, and writing. if you want to study in the united states, it is important to prepare for this test and get a high score.

Negatives and the Simple Present Tense

Good writers can use the negative form of the simple present tense. This section gives you practice with negatives.

Grammar and Sentence Structure

Simple Present Tense Verb Forms: Negatives

Verb *be*	I am **not**	we **are** **not**
	you **are** **not**	you (plural) **are** **not**
	he / she / it **is** **not**	they **are** **not**

NOTE: Some contractions are possible with the verb *be* in negative forms.

is not = isn't	are not = aren't	
For example:	there is not = there isn't	there are not = there aren't

Verb *have*	I **do not** have	we **do not** have
	you **do not** have	you (plural) **do not** have
	he / she / it **does not** have	they **do not** have

Verb *live*	I **do not** live	we **do not** live
	you **do not** live	you (plural) **do not** live
	he / she / it **does not** live	they **do not** live

Verb *go*	I **do not** go	we **do not** go
	you **do not** go	you (plural) **do not** go
	he / she / it **does not** go	they **do not** go

NOTE: Contractions are possible with negative forms of regular verbs.

do not go = don't go   does not go = doesn't go

ACTIVITY 11 Affirmative and Negative Verb Forms

Read the sentences. Change the verb from the positive to the negative. Also write the contraction form. The first one has been done for you.

1. I have a car.

   I do not (don't) have a car.

2. San Juan is in Puerto Rico.

   _____

3. The capital of Japan is Osaka.

   _____

4. Ghaida goes to the library every day.

   _____

5. There is a Thai restaurant on Green Street.

   _____

6. Irene and Julie are roommates.

   _____

7. Charlie works at a gas station.

   _____

8. There are answers in the back of the book.

   _____

9. The teacher wants a new computer.

   _____

10. Aida bakes cookies every Saturday.

   _____

 For more practice with negative simple present tense verbs, try Unit 3, Activity 4 on the *Great Writing 1* Web site: elt.heinle.com/greatwriting

Sentences with Object Pronouns

In Unit 2, you studied subject pronouns. Object pronouns have different forms that you need to learn.

Grammar and Sentence Structure

Object Pronouns

You learned that a pronoun is a word that takes the place of a noun.

After Verbs

An **object pronoun** usually comes after a verb. In English, there are seven object pronouns.

Singular	Plural
me	us
you	you
him / her / it	them

Examples

Singular	Plural
Mona likes <u>me</u>.	Mona likes <u>us</u>.
Do I know <u>you</u>?	Do I know <u>you</u>?
Karen doesn't understand <u>him</u>.	Karen doesn't understand <u>them</u>.

After Prepositions

An object pronoun can also come after a preposition. A **preposition** is a word that shows location, time, or direction. Some common prepositions are *to*, *with*, and *at*. Other prepositions include *on, in, for, by, near, under,* and *from*.

Examples

Singular	Plural
Assad walks **with** <u>me</u>.	Assad walks **with** <u>us</u>.
Can I give the message **to** <u>you</u>?	Can I give the message **to** <u>you</u>?
Jane listens **to** <u>him</u>.	Jane listens **to** <u>them</u>.

Read the following paragraph. Replace the nouns in parentheses with an object pronoun. The first one has been done for you.

EXAMPLE PARAGRAPH 40

My Best Friend

My best friend is Gretchen. I met (**1.** Gretchen) _____*her*_____ ten years ago. She is from Alabama. She comes from a very large family. She has four brothers and three sisters. She doesn't live with (**2.** her brothers and sisters) _____. They live in Alabama with their parents. Gretchen studies veterinary medicine at the University of Florida in Gainesville. She loves (**3.** Gainesville) _____ very much. She also enjoys animals. Gretchen has three pets. She has a cat. She also has a small bird. Gretchen's third pet is a large boa constrictor. She likes (**4.** her pets) _____ all very much. In her free time, Gretchen plays tennis, reads books, and cooks gourmet meals. I love (**5.** Gretchen) _____ like a sister. I hope that our friendship will stay with (**6.** Gretchen and me) _____ for many years.

Sentences with Object Pronouns   **79**

ACTIVITY 13 Possessive Adjective Review: Interviewing a Classmate

Find out the answers to these questions. Ask your classmate. Then write down the answers. Try to use possessive pronouns. Follow the example.

Example: What is your classmate's name? <u>His name is Yoichi.</u>

1. What is your classmate's name? _____

2. Where is your classmate from? _____

3. How big is your classmate's family? _____

4. Why is your classmate in this class? _____

5. What job does your classmate want to do in the future? _____

ACTIVITY 14 Writing Information in Paragraph Form

Write the information about your classmate (from Activity 13) in the form of a paragraph. If you need some help in organization, review Example Paragraph 40 in Activity 12.

EXAMPLE PARAGRAPH 41

_____

_____

_____

_____

_____

_____

_____

_____

_____

_____

Sentence Types: Simple and Compound

All the sentences you have written in the activities up to now have been simple sentences. As you learned in Unit 1, a simple sentence has a subject and a verb. Good writers often combine two simple sentences into one longer sentence. The longer sentence is called a compound sentence.

Sentence Development

Simple and Compound Sentences

Simple Sentences

A **simple sentence** usually has one subject and one verb.

<u>Japan</u> <u>imports</u> oil from Saudi Arabia.

However, a simple sentence can have more than one subject and more than one verb in these combinations:

2 subjects + 1 verb: <u>Japan</u> and <u>Germany</u> <u>import</u> oil from Saudi Arabia.
SUBJECTS   +   VERB

1 subject + 2 verbs: <u>Japan</u> <u>imports</u> oil and <u>exports</u> cars.
SUBJECT   +   VERBS

2 subjects + 2 verbs: <u>Japan</u> and <u>Germany</u> <u>import</u> oil and <u>export</u> cars.
SUBJECTS   +   VERBS

Notice that all of these sentences have one basic subject-verb combination, so they are simple sentences.

Compound Sentences

A **compound sentence** is two sentences joined by a connecting word, such as *and, but,* or *so*. A compound sentence has two subject-verb combinations.

<u>Japan</u> <u>imports</u> oil, and <u>Saudi Arabia</u> <u>imports</u> vegetables.
SUBJECT #1 + VERB #1   SUBJECT #2 + VERB #2

<u>Sue</u> <u>watched</u> TV, so <u>she</u> <u>did not finish</u> her homework.
SUBJECT #1 + VERB #1   SUBJECT #2 + VERB #2

<u>Reju</u> <u>likes</u> to eat Italian food, but <u>he</u> <u>prefers</u> to eat Mexican food.
SUBJECT #1 + VERB #1   SUBJECT #2 + VERB #2

NOTE: Compound sentences *always* use a comma (,) and a connecting word (*and, but, so*) to connect two sentences.

See the Brief Writer's Handbook, pages 226–227, for more connecting words.

Read each sentence. Write S or C to label it as simple or compound. The first two have been done for you. (HINT: Look for the connectors and, but, *or* so *in compound sentences.)*

1. __C__ Japan's flag is red and white, and the Canadian flag is also red and white.

2. __S__ Japan and Canada have the same two colors in their flags.

3. _____ The weather is bad, so the plane cannot take off on time.

4. _____ It is extremely hot in Abu Dhabi during the summer.

5. _____ This map does not include the newly independent countries in Europe or Asia.

6. _____ For less than two hundred dollars, you can buy a round-trip ticket to Boston.

7. _____ The students take a test every Friday, but their scores are not very high.

8. _____ January, March, May, July, August, October, and December have thirty-one days.

9. _____ This recipe requires two cups of flour, two cups of sugar, and one cup of milk.

10. _____ Each ring costs sixty dollars, so five rings cost three hundred dollars.

11. _____ Some people prefer silver rings, but most people prefer gold rings.

12. _____ These silver and gold rings are different in weight and in price.

For more practice with simple versus compound sentences, try Unit 3, Activity 5 and Activity 6 on the *Great Writing 1* Web site: elt.heinle.com/greatwriting

Read each pair of simple sentences. Combine them into one sentence with a comma and a connecting word. Use and, but, *or* so. *Write the compound sentence on the line. Some sentences can be connected with more than one connecting word.*

1. Mary lives in Turkey. Abdul lives in Kuwait.

   _____

2. The weather was cold. I stayed indoors.

   _____

3. We go to school every day. We play tennis on weekends.

   _____

4. Linus and Kathy are related. They are not brother and sister.

   _____

5. The restaurant manager was happy. He gave all the servers a raise.

   _____

✎ **Writer's Note**

Brainstorming *Why* Questions

You use the word *because* to answer a question with *why*. You can put *because* at the beginning or in the middle of a sentence. If you use it at the beginning of a sentence, follow this clause with a comma. *Because* is never used in a simple sentence.

Because Laura felt ill, she went to the doctor.

Laura went to the doctor *because* she felt ill.

Ian ate dinner *because* he was hungry.

(NOTE: See page 156 for more information on *because*.)

Brainstorming with Questions

When you write a paragraph, sometimes it is difficult to find enough information to include. Good writers often ask questions to help them get ideas about what to write. First, think about your topic. Then imagine someone who does not know much about the topic. What questions might that person ask?

Quickly write down as many questions about the topic as you can think of. Do not worry now whether the questions sound good. Your purpose is just to make a list of questions. Later you can go back and read the questions. Then you can decide which questions are good ideas to write about.

Example:

Topic: A popular sport

Possible questions:

1. What is a popular sport?

2. Why is it popular?

3. How many people are needed to play this sport?

4. Is the sport difficult to learn?

5. Where (in which countries) is the sport popular?

6. Is this sport popular on television?

7. How much training does someone need to be good at this sport?

8. How old is this sport?

9. Do you need a lot of equipment to play this sport?

10. Is there a worldwide competition in this sport?

Can you think of other questions?

11. _____

12. _____

The following paragraph about soccer answers some of the questions from the Writer's Note: Brainstorming with Questions. Review the soccer questions and read the paragraph. On the lines below, write the questions that the writer used to create the paragraph.

EXAMPLE PARAGRAPH 42

A Popular Sport

The sport of soccer is the most popular athletic activity in the world. Many people believe that this game comes from England, but others believe that it comes from the Etruscans (a group of people who lived in what is now known as Tuscany in Italy). Soccer is an international phenomenon. People all over the world play and follow this sport. Soccer is popular because it is cheap and fun. It does not require special equipment. It is also fun to watch on television. Every four years, the world enjoys watching the World Cup soccer championship. This time is probably the most exciting time for soccer teams and their fans.

Refer to page 84 for the list of questions:

_____

_____

_____

_____

_____

_____

_____

_____

Grammar and Sentence Structure

Using *A* and *An* with Count Nouns

A **count noun** is a noun that you can count. A count noun has a singular form and a plural form. A non-count noun has only one form.

If you have a singular count noun, use *a* or *an* in front of that noun when it is general (not specific). Use *a* in front of a singular count noun that begins with a consonant sound. Use *an* in front of a singular count noun that begins with a vowel sound.

Forgetting to put *a* or *an* in front of a count noun is a grammatical error. (You will learn more about indefinite articles in Unit 6, pages 151–153.)

NON-COUNT NOUNS	COUNT NOUNS	
	Singular	**Plural**
money	a dollar	twenty dollars
ice	an ice cube	ice cubes
information	a number	numbers
clothing	a blue shirt	blue shirts
vocabulary	a word	fifteen words
bread	a slice of bread	slices of bread
honesty	an honest person	honest people
homework	an assignment	three assignments

ACTIVITY 18 Count and Non-count Nouns

Look at the words listed below. On the line to the left, write C *if the noun is count and* NC *if the noun is non-count. Then circle all the nouns that can be used in this blank: This is* _____. *The first two have been done for you.*

1. __C__ (a cat)   cats   a cats   cat

2. __NC__ a ice   an ice   (ice)   ices

3. _____ moneys   a money   money   a moneys

4. _____ bread   breads   a breads   a bread

5. _____	an eraser	a eraser	erasers	an erasers
6. _____	homeworks	a homework	a homeworks	homework
7. _____	an unit	units	a unit	an units
8. _____	a country	country	an country	a countries
9. _____	information	informations	an information	a information
10. _____	happiness	a happiness	happinesses	an happiness
11. _____	word	a word	words	a words
12. _____	an present	a presents	presents	a present
13. _____	a answer	answers	an answers	an answer
14. _____	politician	politicians	a politician	a politicians

ACTIVITY 19 Editing: Grammar and Sentence Review

Read this paragraph. There are 10 errors: 2 errors with verbs, 1 punctuation error, 2 capitalization errors, 2 adjective errors, 2 possessive adjective errors, and 1 subject pronoun error. Find and correct the errors. The first one has been done for you.

Not an Average Teenager

wants

Steven Mills is not a typical teenager. Steven is a gymnast, and he ~~want~~ to compete in the olympics. He wakes up at five o'clock in the morning every day, because he has to practice before school. First, he has a breakfast healthy. Then she jogs to National Gymnasium on Cypress street. He practices gymnastics for two hours. Then he gets ready for school. Steven goes to school from eight-thirty in the morning until three o'clock in the afternoon. After school, he returns to the gymnasium for classes special with him coach. When practice finish at six o'clock, Steven returns home. He eats dinner, does his homework, and talks with their family. Steven is in bed by ten o'clock so that he will be ready for work the next day.

Building Better Sentences

Correct and varied sentence structure is essential to the quality of your writing. For further practice with the sentences and paragraphs in this unit, go to Practice 3 on pages 234–235 in Appendix 1.

Building Better Vocabulary

ACTIVITY 20 Word Associations

Circle the word or phrase that is most closely related to the word or phrase on the left. If necessary, use a dictionary to check the meaning of words you do not know.

1. free	cheap	no cost
2. entrepreneur	to be the boss	to have a boss
3. part-time	to work thirty hours	to work forty hours
4. engineering	bridges	orchestras
5. typical	rare	normal
6. sibling	uncle	brother
7. forever	no end	an end
8. waiter	restaurant	office
9. to separate	to divide	to mix
10. professional	shorts and a T-shirt	a nice suit
11. to wake up	to stop sleeping	to go to sleep
12. veterinary	people	animals
13. stressful	a picnic	an earthquake
14. athletic	library	soccer field
15. required	must have	optional

ACTIVITY 21 Using Collocations

Fill in each blank with the word on the left that most naturally completes the phrase on the right. If necessary, use a dictionary to check the meaning of words you do not know.

1. common / friendship	to have a _____
2. take / make	to _____ a shower in the morning
3. from / with	to be separated _____ your family
4. small / low	get a _____ score on a test

5.	desk / mistake		a common _____
6.	in / on		to compete _____ a game
7.	in / on		to write _____ the blackboard
8.	of / to		a map _____ the region
9.	ago / after		to meet _____ five years
10.	in / at		to see someone _____ an hour

ACTIVITY 22 Parts of Speech

Study the following word forms. For the sentences on the right, choose the best word and write it in the blank space. Be sure to use the correct form of the verb. If necessary, use a dictionary to check the meaning of words you do not know. (NOTE: The word in bold is the original word that appears in the unit.)

Noun	Verb	Adjective	Sentence Practice
friend/ **friendship** (A PERSON)/ (A THING)	Ø	**friendly**	1. My best _____ lives in Mexico. 2. It is important to be _____ to others.
profession/ professional (A THING)/ (A PERSON)	Ø	**professional**	3. Computer graphics is a popular _____. 4. Her _____ experience is impressive.
separation	separate	**separate**	5. I _____ my clothes before washing them. 6. Joann and her husband drive _____ cars.
visitor/visit (A PERSON)/ (A THING)	**visit**	Ø	7. Wake up! There is a _____ waiting to see you. 8. Every Sunday, Maria _____ her sister.
freedom	free	**free**	9. In college, you have the _____ to choose your major. 10. There is a _____ movie playing tonight.

Noun endings: -ship, -ion, -al, -tion, -or, -dom

Adjective endings: -ly, -al

Original Student Writing

Take a moment to think about your favorite sport. Next, follow these steps for writing. Put a check (✓) next to each step as you complete it. When you finish your paragraph, use the checklist that follows to edit your work. You may want to review What is a Paragraph? *in Unit 2 on page 39.*

STEP 1 _____ In your first sentence, write _____ *is my favorite sport*. Write the name of the sport in the blank space.

STEP 2 _____ In your next sentence, write about the first reason you like the sport. Next, write a sentence with an explanation for this reason.

STEP 3 _____ In the next sentence, write about the second reason that you like the sport. Next, write a sentence with an explanation for this reason.

STEP 4 _____ In the next sentence, write about the reason that you like the sport. Next, write a sentence with an explanation for this reason.

STEP 5 _____ In the last sentence, give your general opinion about this sport.

STEP 6 _____ Use subject pronouns in two of the sentences in STEPS 2 through 4.

STEP 7 _____ Use a possessive adjective in one sentence in STEPS 2 through 4.

STEP 8 _____ Use at least three of the vocabulary words or phrases presented in Activity 20, Activity 21, and Activity 22. Underline these words and phrases in your paragraph.

✓ Checklist

1. ❑ Make sure every sentence has a subject and a verb.

2. ❑ Make sure the verbs are in the correct tense.

3. ❑ Make sure every sentence begins with a capital letter.

4. ❑ Make sure that all the proper nouns (names, cities, countries, etc.) are capitalized.

5. ❑ Make sure every sentence ends with the correct punctuation.

6. ❑ Create a title for your paragraph.

Exchange papers from Activity 23 with a partner. Read your partner's writing. Then use Peer Editing Sheet 3 on page 253 to help you comment on your partner's writing. Be sure to offer positive suggestions and comments that will help your partner improve his or her writing. Consider your partner's comments as you revise your own writing.

Additional Topics for Writing

Here are ten ideas for journal writing. Choose one or more of them to write about. Follow your teacher's directions. (We recommend that you skip a line after each line that you write. This gives your teacher a place to write comments.)

TOPIC 1: Choose a member of your family. Write a paragraph about this person. Include the person's name, age, nationality, job, hobbies, etc.

TOPIC 2: Write about your typical routine for a day of the week. Include the time that you usually wake up, what you eat for breakfast, what your activities are during the day, whom you spend your time with, how you enjoy the day, and what time you go to bed.

TOPIC 3: Write about a special city in a particular country. Include the name of the city, the population, the special tourist attractions, and why it is an important city for you.

TOPIC 4: Write about a job that interests you. Include the title of the job, the duties of the job, and why it is interesting to you.

TOPIC 5: What is your favorite Web site? Write about a Web site that you like. What is the address? What kind of information does it have? Why do you like it?

TOPIC 6: Write about your best friend. What is his/her name? Where does he/she live? What makes your friendship special?

TOPIC 7: Write about a restaurant that you like. What is the name of this restaurant? Why do you like it? What kind of food does it serve? What is the price range? How is it decorated?

TOPIC 8: Write about your favorite movie. What is the title? Who are the main actors in the movie? What is the story about? Why do you like this movie?

TOPIC 9: Write about a specific food that you know how to cook. What are the ingredients? Is it easy to prepare? Are the ingredients expensive?

TOPIC 10: Write about a type of music that you do *not* enjoy. Why don't you like it? How does it make you feel when you hear it?

Timed Writing

How quickly can you write in English? There are many times when you must write quickly—on a test for example. It is important to feel comfortable during those times. Timed-writing practice can make you feel better about writing quickly in English.

Take out a piece of paper. Then read the writing prompt below this paragraph. Your teacher will give you 5 minutes to brainstorm ideas about the topic. You must write 8 to 10 sentences about this topic. You will have 20 minutes to write these sentences. At the end of the 20 minutes, your teacher will collect your work and return it to you later.

> Describe a typical day in your life. What do you normally do? When do you usually do these things?

More Writing

For extra writing practice, see the activities in Unit 8 and Appendix 2.

Writing about the Past

GOAL: To learn how to write sentences in the simple past tense

* **Grammar and Sentence Structure:** Simple past tense of *be* and regular verbs; forming questions; simple past tense of irregular verbs; forming the negative simple past tense of *be*; forming the negative simple past tense of other verbs

* **Sentence Development:** Compound sentences with *but*

Begin with the Simple Past Tense

What happened yesterday? What happened last week? When you talk about actions in the past, you use the **simple past tense**. Both regular verbs and irregular verbs can be used in the simple past tense.

Grammar and Sentence Structure

Simple Past Tense: Statements and Questions

Simple Past Tense of Be: *Statements*

The most common verb in English, *be*, is an irregular verb. Study the simple past tense form of the verb *be*.

Verb *be*	I **was**	we **were**
	you **were**	you (plural) **were**
	he / she / it **was**	they **were**

Incorrect:	I am in Guatemala last year.
Incorrect:	I were in Guatemala last year.
Correct:	I was in Guatemala last year.

Simple Past Tense of Be: Questions

To form questions with the verb *be* in the simple past tense, switch the subject and the verb. Study the forms below.

Verb *be*	**Was** I . . . ?	**Were** we . . . ?
	Were you . . . ?	**Were** you (plural) . . . ?
	Was he / she / it . . . ?	**Were** they . . . ?

Incorrect:	**Was** Khalid and Mario at the mall yesterday?
Incorrect:	**Khalid and Mario were** at the mall yesterday?
Correct:	**Were** Khalid and Mario at the mall yesterday?

Simple Past Tense of Regular Verbs: Statements

Forming the simple past of regular verbs is easy. Just add *-ed* or *-d* to the ends of regular verbs. (See the Brief Writer's Handbook, pages 218–219, for more about the spelling of regular simple past tense verbs.) Study the examples below.

Verb *live*	I **lived**	we **lived**
	you **lived**	you (plural) **lived**
	he / she / it **lived**	they **lived**

Verb *visit*	I **visited**	we **visited**
	you **visited**	you (plural) **visited**
	he / she / it **visited**	they **visited**

Incorrect:	We **call** our parents yesterday.
Correct:	We **called** our parents yesterday.

Simple Past Tense of Regular Verbs: Questions

To form questions with regular verbs in the simple past tense, use this form:
did + subject + base form of main verb (no *-ed/–d*!).

NOTE: *Did* shows that the sentence is in the *simple past* tense and that it is a *question*. Be sure to use the <u>base form</u> (not the simple past) of the main verb.

Verb *live*	**Did** I **live** . . . ?	**Did** we **live** . . . ?
	Did you **live** . . . ?	**Did** you (plural) **live** . . . ?
	Did he / she / it **live** . . . ?	**Did** they **live** . . . ?

Incorrect:	Did the tourists **hiked** down the mountain last night?
Incorrect:	**Do** the tourists hike down the mountain last night?
Incorrect:	**The tourists hiked** down the mountain last night?
Correct:	Did the tourists hike down the mountain last night?

✏ Writer's Note

Time Phrases with the Simple Past Tense

We use certain words and phrases in a sentence to help show that something happened in the past. Some of these time phrases include:

last night   last week   this morning   yesterday   (two minutes) ago

You can put these time phrases at the beginning or the end of a sentence. Avoid using them in the middle of a sentence. Study these examples. Can you think of any others?

Incorrect: I yesterday scratched my knee.

Correct: Yesterday I scratched my knee.

Correct: I scratched my knee yesterday.

Incorrect: Did Maria last night go to the party?

Correct: Did Maria go to the party last night?

ACTIVITY 1 Sentences with the Simple Past Tense

The verbs in these sentences are in the simple present tense. Rewrite the sentences and change the verbs to the simple past tense. The first sentence has been done for you.

1. Mary and her daughter Natalie visit the farm.

   Mary and her daughter Natalie visited the farm.

2. Mary and Natalie play with many animals.

   _____

3. They laugh at the animals.

   _____

4. Natalie really enjoys herself.

   _____

5. She likes the chickens best.

   _____

6. Natalie watches them play all morning.

   _____

7. They play with the baby goats.

   _____

8. Finally, they return home.

   _____

For more practice with the simple present tense and simple past tense of regular verbs, try Unit 4, Activity 1 on the *Great Writing 1* Web site: elt.heinle.com/greatwriting

ACTIVITY 2 More Work with the Simple Past Tense

Read the paragraph and circle the ten simple past tense verbs. When you finish, answer the questions in complete sentences. The first one has been done for you.

EXAMPLE PARAGRAPH 44

Lao-Tzu and Taoism

Lao-Tzu (was) an important **philosopher**. He was born in China. He lived in the Hunan **province**, and he worked as a court **librarian**. The government in Hunan was **corrupt**, so Lao-Tzu decided to leave his home. Before he **abandoned** the province, someone asked him to write a book about how to live correctly. He agreed to write the book *Tao Te Ching*. These ideas were the beginning of the philosophy of Taoism.

a philosopher: a person who studies the universe, nature, life, and morals
a province: a territory in a country

a librarian: someone who works with books
corrupt: dishonest
abandoned: left (He left the province.)

Information for this paragraph came from Microsoft Encarta 96 and *Simple Abundance: A Daybook of Comfort and Joy* by Sarah Ban Breathnach, published by Warner Books, Inc., 1995.

1. Who was Lao-Tzu?

   Lao-Tzu was a famous philosopher.

2. Where was he born?

   _____

3. What was his job?

   _____

4. What did he do before he left his home?

   _____

5. What did this book create?

   _____

96   UNIT 4 • Writing about the Past

ACTIVITY 3 An Important Person

Think of an important person who lived in the past. It could be someone famous in history. It could be a famous singer, politician, or athlete. It could be someone from your family. (However, this person should not be alive.) Answer the questions using complete sentences.

1. Who was this person?

   _____

2. Where was the person born?

   _____

3. What was the person's job?

   _____

4. Why is the person important to you? What did he or she do?

   _____

   _____

   _____

   _____

   _____

5. How do you feel when you think about this person? Why?

   _____

   _____

   _____

   _____

Read the paragraph. Circle all of the simple past tense verbs. Then follow the directions and make changes to the paragraph. The first sentence has been done for you. (You may want to review subject pronouns and possessive adjectives in Unit 2.)

EXAMPLE PARAGRAPH 45

The Top of the Class

In 2002, Antonio and Marcus (were) the top students at the University of North Carolina.

They studied in the history department. They excelled in their studies. In class, they answered all

of their instructors' questions. Their test grades beat the other students', and their class projects

received excellent marks. When they graduated in 2006, they finished at the top of the class. All

of the teachers were very proud of Antonio and Marcus.

Rewrite the paragraph on the lines below and make these changes:

1. Change *Antonio and Marcus* to *Fatima*. (NOTE: *Fatima* is a woman's name.)

2. Change the underlined pronouns to go with *Fatima*.

3. Change any other words necessary (such as *students* to *student* in the first sentence).

The Top of the Class

In 2002, Fatima was the top student at the University of North Carolina.

_____

_____

_____

_____

_____

_____

_____

_____

_____

_____

_____

For more practice with plural and singular, try Unit 4, Activity 2 on the *Great Writing 1* Web site: elt.heinle.com/greatwriting

First, discuss these questions with your classmates.

1. How do deaf people communicate with each other?

2. How do blind people read?

3. Do you know anyone who is both deaf and blind?

Then read the paragraph. Answer the questions below using forms of be. *Use complete sentences. The first one has been done for you.*

EXAMPLE PARAGRAPH 47

Helen Keller (1880–1968)

Helen Keller was a famous American author. She was born healthy. However, when she was two years old, she became very ill. The illness made her **deaf** and **blind**. She could not communicate with anyone. When she was seven years old, a teacher taught her how to communicate. The teacher's name was Annie Sullivan. When Helen was twenty years old, she started college. After her graduation, she wrote thirteen books and traveled around the world. She was an incredible human being.

deaf: not able to hear
blind: not able to see

1. What was the blind and deaf person's name?

   <u>The blind and deaf person's name was Helen Keller.</u>

2. What country was she from?

   _____

3. Was she healthy or unhealthy when she was born?

   _____

4. How old was she when she became ill?

   _____

5. Who was her teacher?

_____

6. How old was she when she learned to communicate?

_____

7. How old was she when she went to college?

_____

8. What kind of person was Helen Keller?

_____

Irregular Simple Past Tense Verbs

In this unit, you learned how to make the simple past tense of a regular verb—add *-ed* or *-d* to the base form of the verb. Some verbs, however, are irregular. This means that they take a different form in the simple past tense.

Grammar and Sentence Structure

Simple Past Tense of Irregular Verbs

Here are some common irregular verbs. (See the Brief Writer's Handbook, page 220, for a complete list of common irregular simple past tense verbs.)

be	→ was/were	feel	→ felt	pay → paid	send → sent
buy	→ bought	go	→ went	run → ran	sit → sat
cut	→ cut	have	→ had	ride → rode	speak → spoke
do	→ did	leave	→ left	say → said	teach → taught
draw	→ drew	make	→ made	see → saw	write → wrote

NOTE: To form questions with irregular verbs, follow the rules for regular verbs on page 94. Use *did* and the simple (base) form of the verb.

There is no special rule that tells when a verb is irregular. You must memorize the simple past tense form when you learn the word. A dictionary will tell you when a verb is irregular. Now study these sentences for correct forms of the irregular simple past tense in statements and in questions.

Incorrect:	Last night, I **buy** a new CD.
Incorrect:	Last night, I **buyed** a new CD.
Correct:	Last night, I bought a new CD.
Incorrect:	Did you **left** your dictionary at home?
Incorrect:	**Do** you **left** your dictionary at home?
Correct:	Did you leave your dictionary at home?

ACTIVITY 6 Irregular Simple Past Tense Verbs

Answer the following questions. Use the irregular form of the simple past tense. Use verbs from the list in Grammar and Sentence Structure: Simple Past Tense of Irregular Verbs on page 101. The first one has been done for you.

1. Where were you last summer?

   I was in Dubai.

2. How did you feel yesterday?

3. Where did you go last weekend?

4. When did you see a funny movie?

5. What did you buy last week?

6. Whom did you speak with yesterday?

7. When did you leave for school this morning?

8. When did you do your homework?

9. Where did you eat lunch yesterday?

10. When did you last send an e-mail?

 For more practice with the simple present tense and simple past tense of irregular verbs, try Unit 4, Activity 3 and Activity 4 on the *Great Writing 1* Web site: elt.heinle.com/greatwriting

Grammar and Sentence Structure

Making *Be* Negative

When you want to make a negative sentence with *be*, you use the word *not*. *Not* comes after the form of *be*.

Paula was <u>not</u> home   The CDs were <u>not</u> in their cases.

See Grammar and Sentence Structure—Simple Past Tense: Statements and Questions on pages 93–94 for a review of the forms of *be*.

Simple Past Tense Verb Forms: Negatives

Verb *be*	I **was not**		we **were not**
	you **were not**		you (plural) **were not**
	he / she / it **was not**		they **were not**

NOTE: Some contractions are possible with the verb *be* in negative form.

was not = wasn't   were not = weren't

Careful! Be sure that the apostrophe (') is placed directly before the letter *t*. Remember that the apostrophe in negatives takes the place of the missing letter.

Incorrect:	She **is'nt** my sister.
Incorrect:	She **isn,t** my sister.
Correct:	She isn't my sister. (Or: She's not my sister.)
Incorrect:	I **was'nt** in class yesterday.
Incorrect:	I **wasn,t** in class yesterday.
Correct:	I wasn't in class yesterday.

✏ Writer's Note

Using Contractions

It is important to remember that contractions might be too informal for academic writing. Ask your instructor if using contractions in this course is acceptable.

Read the following paragraph. Write the correct form of the be *verb in the blanks. Be sure to use the negative form where indicated. The first one has been done for you.*

Moving to the United States

My name is Panadda, and I (**1.**) _____was_____ born in Thailand. I (**2.** negative)

_____ the first child. My sister Suntri (**3.**) _____ born three years

before I (**4.**) _____ born. My parents (**5.** negative) _____ rich, but they

(**6.**) _____ always happy. They (**7.**) _____ hard workers. In 1999,

we moved to the United States. Everyone in my family (**8.**) _____ very excited.

We (**9.**) _____ also scared. My parents (**10.** negative) _____ able to

speak English. When we arrived, they began English classes. My sister and I started school.

We (**11.** negative) _____ comfortable in the classroom because we did not know

the language. After a few years, we learned the language and the culture of the United States.

ACTIVITY 8 Improving Your Own Writing

Turn to page 3 and look at Activity 2. Read your sentences again. Can you make these sentences better? Try to change the sentences to the simple past tense. Add three more sentences about your family. Make the sentences into a simple paragraph. Write your changes on the lines below. Use Example Paragraph 48 in Activity 7 as a guide.

_____

_____

_____

_____

_____

_____

_____

_____

_____

Grammar and Sentence Structure

Other Negative Verbs

Aside from the verb *be*, the negative form of all other verbs in English is formed in the same way in the simple past tense. Just write *did not* and the simple (base) form of the verb. Look at these examples.

Verb *live* (negative past)

I **did not live**	we **did not live**
you **did not live**	you (plural) **did not live**
he / she / it **did not live**	they **did not live**

NOTE: Contraction: *did not = didn't*

Incorrect: Ahmed **no finish** his homework.

Incorrect: Ahmed **no finished** his homework.

Correct: Ahmed did not (didn't) finish his homework.

ACTIVITY 9 Practicing Negative Verbs in the Simple Past

The words in the sentences below are not in the correct order. First, make the verbs negative. Then write the words in the correct order to make correct English sentences. The first one has been done for you.

1. lived (negative) / . / in Johannesburg in 2002 / Carmen

    Carmen did not live in Johannesburg in 2002.

2. Ling / engineering / . / studied (negative)

    _____

3. last year / him / Humberto's parents / visited (negative) / .

    _____

4. large brains / had (negative) / . / Dinosaurs

    _____

5. ! / John / helped (negative) / me / with my homework

    _____

6. Edda / the letter / . / sent (negative) / to her parents

    _____

7. spoke (negative) / . / Karl / with his parents / last night

    _____

8. I / my homework / did (negative) / . / yesterday

_____

9. Janiel and Yosemy / last night / . / left (negative) / the party early

_____

10. went (negative) / My brother / to the grocery store / last Saturday / .

_____

 For more practice with negative verbs in the simple past, try Unit 4, Activity 5 on the *Great Writing 1* Web site: elt.heinle.com/greatwriting

Simple Past Tense Review

In this unit, you learned about simple past tense verbs, questions, and negatives. The next activities will help you review what you have learned.

ACTIVITY 10 Editing: Writing Negative Simple Past Sentences

The sentences below are false. Work with a partner and rewrite each sentence using the negative form of the verb to make the sentence true. Then write a correct sentence. Follow the example. Some verbs are regular and some are irregular. Refer to the complete list of irregular verbs in the Brief Writer's Handbook, page 220.

1. Tony Blair was a leader of Mexico.

   Tony Blair was not a leader of Mexico. He was a leader of Great Britain.

2. Confucius lived in Japan.

   _____

3. Pelé played basketball.

   _____

4. In the 1980s, Madonna sang in Arabic.

   _____

5. The *Titanic* sank in the Pacific Ocean.

   _____

6. The Statue of Liberty came from Italy.

_____

7. The Wright Brothers invented the radio.

_____

8. Stephen King wrote *Romeo and Juliet.*

_____

ACTIVITY 11 Simple Past Tense Review

Read the following paragraph. Change the verbs in parentheses to the simple past tense. Write the negative form where indicated. The first one has been done for you.

EXAMPLE PARAGRAPH 49

Bob's Horrible Day

Bob (**1.** have) _____*had*_____ a horrible day on Monday. First, he (**2.** be) _____

supposed to get up at 6 A.M., but his alarm clock (**3.** work, negative) _____. He

(**4.** wake up) _____ at 8 A.M. There (**5.** be, negative) _____

any hot water for a shower, so he had to use cold water. After that, his car (**6.** start, negative)

_____, and he had to take the bus. When Bob (**7.** get) _____ to work,

his boss (**8.** yell) _____ at him for being late. Next, his computer (**9.** crash)

_____, and he (**10.** lose) _____ all of his documents. He (**11.** stay)

_____ at work until midnight to redo the documents. Bob (**12.** decide)

_____ to stay home the next day because he (**13.** be) _____ too tired

from all his bad luck.

For more practice with reviewing the simple past tense, try Unit 4, Activity 6 on the *Great Writing 1* Web site: elt.heinle.com/greatwriting

Compound Sentences with *But*

One common sentence connector is *but*. This word is often used to make compound sentences. The connector *but* shows a contrast.

Sentence Development

Compound Sentences with *But*

The connector *but* indicates a contrast between the ideas it connects. Study this example.

Two simple sentences: I bought a car. John bought a truck.
One compound sentence: I bought a car, *but* John bought a truck.

This example is a compound sentence because it is two complete sentences connected by the word *but*. It has two separate subject-verb combinations.

I <u>bought</u> a car, but <u>John</u> <u>bought</u> a truck.
SUBJ. VERB   SUBJ.   VERB

Look at another example.

Two simple sentences: She studied for the exam. She did not pass it.
One compound sentence: She studied for the exam, *but* she did not pass it.

NOTE: Notice the comma before *but*. You must put a comma before a connector in a compound sentence.

NOTE: Sometimes *but* is not a connector. In these cases, it is a preposition that means the same as the word *except*. Notice that there is no comma before *but*. Consider these examples:

<u>We</u> <u>visited</u> all of the countries in South America *but* Chile.
SUBJ.   VERB

<u>All</u> of the new cars *but* this one <u>are</u> luxury cars.
SUBJ.   VERB

These two sentences are simple sentences. There is only one subject-verb combination in each sentence.

ACTIVITY 12 Compound Sentence Review

Read the following sentences. Some are compound sentences, and some are simple sentences. First, identify the type of sentence as S (simple) or C (compound). If the sentence is compound, insert a comma where it is necessary. The first three have been done for you.

1. ___S___ The girls practiced every day.

2. ___S___ They did not win the tennis tournament.

3. ___C___ The girls practiced every day, but they did not win the tennis tournament.

4. _____ The committee members made a decision but the manager did not like it.

5. _____ Neal worked with his father at the shoe store for almost twenty years.

6. _____ We went to Canada but we did not visit Toronto.

7. _____ With the recent increase in crime in that area of the city, the local residents there are worried about their safety.

8. _____ Summer is a good time to practice outdoor sports but winter is not.

9. _____ All of the workers but Marian arrived at yesterday's income tax meeting on time.

10. _____ Saudi Arabia and Kuwait import equipment, cars, food, and medicine.

11. _____ The chairs in the living room are made of pine but the chairs in my office are made of oak.

12. _____ All of the chairs in the kitchen but this one are made of maple.

ACTIVITY 13 Writing Compound Sentences

Read these charts. They give information about two brothers.

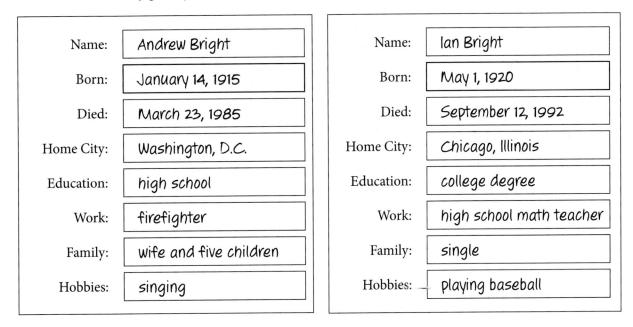

Now read the incorrect statements below about the brothers. Then write a compound sentence with but. *Use the information in the charts. The first one has been done for you.*

1. They were born on the same day.

   Andrew was born on January 14, but Ian was born on May 1. _____

2. The brothers were born in the same year.

   _____

3. They both sang as a hobby.

   _____

4. Both brothers were married.

_____

5. They lived in the same city.

_____

6. They had the same level of education.

_____

7. Both men had the same kind of job.

_____

8. They died on the same date.

_____

ACTIVITY 14 Interviewing Your Classmates

Walk around the classroom and ask different classmates the following questions. Write down the answers. When you have finished, write complete sentences using information about yourself and the information you received from your classmates. The first one has been done for you.

1. Where are you from? *Classmate's answer:* Peru _____

   I am from Kuwait, but José is from Peru. _____

2. What did you eat for dinner last night? *Classmate's answer:* _____

   _____

3. Where was your last vacation? *Classmate's answer:* _____

   _____

4. Why did you come to this school? *Classmate's answer:* _____

   _____

5. What country do you want to visit? *Classmate's answer:* _____

   _____

 For more practice with compound sentences using *but*, try Unit 4, Activity 7 on the *Great Writing 1* Web site: elt.heinle.com/greatwriting

Read the following paragraph. Find and correct the 14 errors. If you need some help locating the errors, look at the numbers in parentheses on the left. This number tells you how many errors are in each line. The first one has been done for you.

EXAMPLE PARAGRAPH 50

Muhammad Ibn Batuta

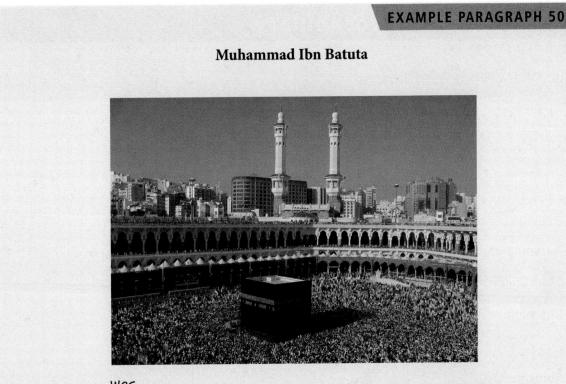

(3)   Ibn Batuta ^was^ a famous moroccan traveler. He live in Morocco in the fourteenth century.

(2)   When he was a man young, he made a religious trip to Mecca. However, Ibn Batuta loves to

(2)   see new places so much that he continued to travel. This was no his original plan but he

(2)   continued on his journey. He had many adventures during her travels and he met many

(1)   interesting people. After he returned home, he did not forgot about his journey. He wrote a

(2)   book about his travels, this book now gives us a lot of information important about life in the

(2)   fourteenth century. Also gives us more information about this interesting and important man

Building Better Sentences

Correct and varied sentence structure is essential to the quality of your writing. For further practice with the sentences and paragraphs in this unit, go to Practice 4 on page 235 in Appendix 1.

Building Better Vocabulary

ACTIVITY 16 Word Associations

Circle the word or phrase that is most closely related to the word or phrase on the left. If necessary, use a dictionary to check the meaning of words you do not know.

1.	horrible	very bad news	very good news
2.	century	ten years	one hundred years
3.	to communicate	to share information	to keep information
4.	excellent	the worst	the best
5.	to continue	to pause	to not stop
6.	proud	grade of 45%	grade of 100%
7.	province	region	project
8.	librarian	books	cars
9.	separate	together	apart
10.	to graduate	to complete work	to complete school
11.	beginning	initial	final
12.	manager	boss	teacher
13.	original	a copy	not a copy
14.	to arrive	to come to a place	to leave a place
15.	to scare	to laugh	to scream

Fill in each blank with the word on the left that most naturally completes the phrase on the right. If necessary, use a dictionary to check the meaning of words you do not know.

1. before / first   the _____ thing to do

2. to / for   a trip _____ Puerto Rico

3. to / at   arrive _____ the supermarket

4. information / communication   share _____ about the problem

5. about / for   have a question _____ your homework

6. abandon / excel   _____ all hope

7. take / make   _____ a decision

8. excellence / communication   effective _____

9. freedom / beginning   the _____ to do anything that you want to do

10. supposed / excited   be _____ about a new class

Study the following word forms. For the sentences on the right, choose the best word and write it in the blank space. Be sure to use the correct form of the verb. If necessary, use a dictionary to check the meaning of words you do not know. (NOTE: The word in bold is the original word that appears in the unit.)

Noun	Verb	Adjective	Sentence Practice
pride	Ø	**proud**	1. She was very _____ when she graduated.
			2. I have a lot of _____ in my children.
excell<u>ence</u>	**excel**	**excellent**	3. Damon _____ in swimming when he was younger.
			4. That was an _____ movie!
communica<u>tion</u>	**communicate**	communica<u>tive</u>	5. We _____ for three hours by phone yesterday.
			6. Roberto was shy, but now he is more _____.
continua<u>tion</u>	**continue**	continu<u>ous</u>/ continu<u>al</u>	7. The students _____ to study after the semester ended.
			8. The _____ traffic noise gave me a headache.
culture	Ø	cultur<u>al</u>	9. Do you know about Indian _____?
			10. Kim and Jo's _____ differences are small.

Noun endings: -ence, -ion, -tion

Adjective endings: -ive, -ous, -al

Original Student Writing

Reread the paragraph about Lao-Tzu on page 96 and your answers to Activity 3 on page 97. You will use this kind of information to write in the simple past tense about an important person.

Think of an important person. Then follow these steps for writing. Put a check (✓) next to each step as you complete it. When you finish your paragraph, use the checklist that follows to edit your work. Remember to write in the simple past tense. You may want to review What Is a Paragraph? *in Unit 2 on page 39.*

Step 1 _____ In your first sentence, tell the name of the person and how that person was important.

Step 2 _____ In your next sentence, write where the person was born.

Step 3 _____ In the next sentence, tell about the person's job.

Step 4 _____ In the next three or four sentences, tell a short story about the person. The story should show why the person is important.

Step 5 _____ Try to use the word *but* in one of the sentences in Step 4. Remember to use a comma!

Step 6 _____ Use a <u>negative</u> verb in one of the sentences in Step 4.

Step 7 _____ In the last sentence, write why you chose this person.

Step 8 _____ Use at least three of the vocabulary words or phrases presented in Activity 16, Activity 17, and Activity 18. Underline these words and phrases in your paragraph.

✔ Checklist

1. ❑ Make sure every sentence has a subject and a verb.

2. ❑ Make sure the verbs are the correct form of the simple past tense.

3. ❑ Make sure every sentence begins with a capital letter.

4. ❑ Make sure that all the proper nouns (names, cities, countries, etc.) are capitalized.

5. ❑ Make sure every sentence ends with the correct punctuation.

6. ❑ Create a title for your paragraph.

Exchange papers from Activity 19 with a partner. Read your partner's writing. Then use Peer Editing Sheet 4 on page 255 to help you comment on your partner's writing. Be sure to offer positive suggestions and comments that will help your partner improve his or her writing. Consider your partner's comments as you revise your own writing.

Additional Topics for Writing

Here are ten ideas for journal writing. Choose one or more of them to write about. Follow your teacher's directions. (We recommend that you skip a line after each line that you write. This gives your teacher a place to write comments.)

TOPIC 1: Describe a vacation you took. Where did you go? What did you do? Who went on this vacation with you? How old were you when you went on this trip? Did you like this vacation?

TOPIC 2: Describe a home you lived in when you were a child. How big was the house? What color was the house? Where was the house? Did you like the house? What was your favorite room in the house?

TOPIC 3: Write about a movie you saw or a book you read. Did you like it? Who was your favorite character? What was the story about? Did the author have a message for the audience of this book or movie?

TOPIC 4: Write about what you did last weekend. Where did you go? Who did you go with? Did you enjoy it?

TOPIC 5: Write about a person you used to know. Who was this person? Where did you meet this person? What was special about this person?

TOPIC 6: Write about an important event in your life. How old were you? What happened? Why is this event important to you?

TOPIC 7: Describe a holiday that you and your family spent together. What was the occasion? Which family members were there? What did you do?

TOPIC 8: Write about something embarrassing that happened to you. How old were you? What happened? Why were you embarrassed? Who saw this happen? How did you feel afterwards?

TOPIC 9: Write about a day you spent outdoors. What did you do? Where did you go? Who did you go with? What specific activities did you do? How was the weather?

TOPIC 10: Describe a pet you had in the past. What was the pet's name? What kind of animal was it? How long did you have this pet? Why did you like this pet? (*Or:* Why did you dislike this pet?)

Timed Writing

How quickly can you write in English? There are many times when you must write quickly—on a test for example. It is important to feel comfortable during those times. Timed-writing practice can make you feel better about writing quickly in English.

Take out a piece of paper. Then read the writing prompt below this paragraph. Your teacher will give you 5 minutes to brainstorm ideas about the topic. You must write 8 to 10 sentences about this topic. You will have 20 minutes to write these sentences. At the end of the 20 minutes, your teacher will collect your work and return it to you later.

> Describe a sad (or happy, frightening, funny, important, etc.) event or time from your past. What was the event or time? Give examples of how this event or time made you feel that emotion.

More Writing

For extra writing practice, see the activities in Unit 8 and Appendix 2.

Describing Actions

GOAL: To learn how to write sentences in the present progressive tense

***Grammar and Sentence Structure:** Present progressive tense; adverbs of manner

***Sentence Development:** Compound sentences with *and*; compound sentences with *so*

Using the Present Progressive

When good writers write about actions that are happening at the moment, they often use the present progressive tense.

Grammar and Sentence Structure

Present Progressive Tense for Current Actions

The **present progressive tense** (*be* + verb + *-ing*) is often used to describe actions that are happening right now. Review the chart below before beginning the activities in this unit. (See the Brief Writer's Handbook, page 221, for spelling rules of verbs ending in *-ing*.)

Present Progressive Tense

I	am eat**ing**	we	are eat**ing**
you	are eat**ing**	you (plural)	are eat**ing**
he / she / it	is eat**ing**	they	are eat**ing**
I	am walk**ing**	we	are walk**ing**
you	are walk**ing**	you (plural)	are walk**ing**
he / she / it	is walk**ing**	they	are walk**ing**

Be careful! Some verbs in English do *not* usually take the progressive tense because they are not action verbs. Here are some common stative, or non-action, verbs: *be, have, see, love, believe, own,* and *want.* (See the Brief Writer's Handbook, page 222, for more information.)

Read the following paragraph about a Sunday afternoon at the zoo. Underline all the present progressive verbs. There are 16.

A Day Trip for the Jimenez Family

The Jimenez family lives in Puerto Rico. It is a large family with Mr. and Mrs. Jimenez, their two sons Javier and Pablo, and their daughter Rosario. Today is an interesting day for the Jimenez family. They are visiting the Mayaguez Zoo. Mr. Jimenez and Rosario love monkeys, so they are walking around the monkey **exhibit**. They are watching the chimpanzees and orangutans. The chimps are playing with each other, and some of them are swinging from ropes. The monkeys look like they are having a good time. One orangutan is looking at the **crowd** of people. The other orangutan is eating a banana. At the other end of the zoo, the rest of the Jimenez family is walking around the lion exhibit. Javier and Pablo are talking about how strong the male lion looks. This big lion is walking around and **yawning**. Mrs. Jimenez is talking to her sons. She is telling a story about a **safari** that she took when she was younger. Javier and Pablo are listening to their mother's story, and they are asking Mrs. Jimenez to take them on a safari.

an exhibit: a display, a performance
a crowd: a large group (of people)

yawning: opening its mouth to show sleepiness
a safari: a trip to observe wild animals, particularly in East Africa

Study the picture of the soccer game. Read the prompts that are connected to each action. Complete the sentences on the next page using the present progressive tense.

Other fans / wave / flags and banners

Some fans / cheer / for their team

The coach / watch / the ball

The referee / run / toward the goal

The soccer ball / go / into the net

The forward / hope / the shot will be a goal

The goalkeeper / jump / for the ball

1. The soccer ball _____.

2. The goalkeeper _____.

3. The coach _____.

4. The referee _____.

5. The forward _____.

6. Some fans _____.

7. Other fans _____.

After you complete the sentences, compare them to a classmate's sentences.

ACTIVITY 3 Writing a Paragraph

Rewrite the sentences from Activity 2 in paragraph form. Try to use your imagination and add some extra information and adjectives about this game. Create a title for the paragraph.

EXAMPLE PARAGRAPH 52

_____

   The soccer game between Blackwatch and the Stingers is very exciting. Many things are happening right now! _____

_____

_____

_____

_____

_____

_____

_____

_____

Study the picture of Bruce and his friends. Then read the paragraph. Fill in the missing verbs based on what you see in the picture.

A University Student's Room

Tomorrow is a big day for Bruce. His mother is coming to visit him at college for the first time.

Bruce is very excited, but he is also worried. His dorm room is a mess. This is why he called all his

friends to come help him. His good friend Lina (**1.**) _____ the floor

because the carpet is very dirty. Bruce's friend Joe (**2.**) _____

some of Bruce's clothes to the laundry. At the same time, Bruce's roommate Paul

(**3.**) _____ all of the empty pizza boxes and soda cans. Bruce

(**4.**) _____. Bruce feels very lucky to have such good friends, and he

is sure that the room will be ready for his mother's visit.

For more practice with the present progressive tense, try Unit 5, Activity 1 on the *Great Writing 1* Web site: elt.heinle.com/greatwriting

Using the Connector *And*

In Unit 4, you practiced using the connector *but* to make compound sentences. In the following activities, you will practice another common connector—*and*.

Sentence Development

Compound Sentences with *And*

Good writers often use the connector *and* to join words and ideas. Here are some common examples.

1. **And is used to join two (or more) words that are in the same grammar category (or group).**

    Example A: In the following sentence, *and* joins two <u>nouns</u> and makes the subject of the sentence plural.

    > Bobby *and* Jenny go to Oak Ridge Elementary School.

    This sentence combines these two ideas:

    > Bobby goes to Oak Ridge Elementary School.

    > Jenny goes to Oak Ridge Elementary School.

    Example B: In the following sentence, *and* joins two <u>nouns</u> and makes the object of the sentence plural.

    > My sister loves pizza *and* spaghetti.

    This sentence combines these two ideas:

    > My sister loves pizza.

    > My sister loves spaghetti.

    Example C: In the following sentence, *and* joins two <u>verbs</u> in a sentence.

    > Ricardo works *and* studies at the university.

    This sentence combines these two ideas:

    > Ricardo works at the university.

    > Ricardo studies at the university.

    Example D: In the following sentence, *and* joins two <u>adjectives</u> in a sentence.

    > The weather was hot *and* muggy.

    This sentence combines these two ideas:

    > The weather was hot.

    > The weather was muggy.

2. **The connector *and* is also used to form compound sentences.** Remember from Unit 3 that a compound sentence is two sentences joined by a comma and a connecting word. A compound sentence has two subject-verb combinations.

    Example A:

    > Irene works at the mall, *and* her brother visits her store every day.

This sentence combines these two sentences:

Irene works at the mall.

Irene's brother visits her store every day.

NOTE: When you join these two sentences, you do not need to repeat *Irene* after the connector. You can use the possessive adjective *her*.

Example B:

Joanna is washing the car, *and* her mother is cooking dinner.

This sentence combines these two sentences:

Joanna is washing the car.

Joanna's mother is cooking dinner.

ACTIVITY 5 Compound Sentence Practice

Read the two lists of sentences. Match a sentence from Column A with a sentence from Column B. Then write a compound sentence using and *on the lines below. The first one has been done for you.*

Column A	Column B
~~John is watching a movie.~~	Milk has a large amount of vitamin D.
Oranges contain a lot of vitamin C.	I hope they will grow quickly.
Bolivia is a landlocked country in South America.	~~Ann is doing her homework.~~
That blouse is the perfect color for you.	Ajman is a part of the United Arab Emirates.
I am planting marigold seeds.	She hopes they will arrive on time.
Arizona is a part of the United States.	It matches your pants and your handbag.
Valia is having guests for dinner tonight.	Switzerland is a landlocked country in Europe.

1. John is watching a movie, and Ann is doing her homework.

2. _____

3. _____

4. _____

5. _____

6. _____

7. _____

ACTIVITY 6 Analyzing Compound Sentences with *And*

Read the paragraph and complete the sentence analysis that follows.

EXAMPLE PARAGRAPH 54

Jobs for the Future

Canan and Seher are studying engineering at Istanbul University. The two women are cousins. Canan lives with her family, and Seher stays with her uncle's family. They are going to graduate at the end of the year. Both Canan and Seher want to get good jobs in the private sector when they graduate. Canan hopes to work for a large international company, and Seher wants to get a job with the local electric company.

Now read each sentence below. Rewrite the information using two sentences instead of one. The first one has been done for you.

1. Canan and Seher are studying engineering at Istanbul University.

   Meaning: <u>Canan is studying engineering at Istanbul University.</u>

   <u>Seher is studying engineering at Istanbul University.</u>

2. Canan lives with her family, and Seher stays with her uncle's family.

   Meaning: _____

   _____

3. They are going to graduate at the end of the year.

   Meaning: _____

   _____

4. Both Canan and Seher want to get good jobs in the private sector when they graduate.

   Meaning: _____

   _____

5. Canan hopes to work for a large international company, and Seher wants to get a job with the local electric company.

   Meaning: _____

   _____

For more practice with compound sentences, try Unit 5, Activity 2 on the *Great Writing 1* Web site: elt.heinle.com/greatwriting

Using the Connector *And*   **125**

Using the Connector *So*

So is another connector that good writers use in compound sentences. This connector shows a cause and a result.

Sentence Development

Compound Sentences with *So*

The connector *so* shows a result. The first subject-verb combination gives the "cause," and the second subject-verb combination gives the "result."

(CAUSE)   (RESULT)
I was hungry, <u>so</u> I ate a sandwich.

(CAUSE)   (RESULT)
Leslie has a big exam tomorrow, <u>so</u> she is studying at the library.

(CAUSE)   (RESULT)
The children had a long day, <u>so</u> they are taking a nap now.

NOTE: Another word for a subject-verb combination is a **clause**. In each example above, there are two clauses. These sentences are compound. Remember to use a comma before *so* when it shows cause and result.

NOTE: When *so* is a connector in a compound sentence, we use a comma. However, *so* has several other meanings. Study these three additional meanings. A comma is not possible with these other meanings.

1. so = an adverb that means *very* or *extremely*

   It is so hot today.

   You speak English so well.

2. so = a connector that means *in order to*; it is a short form for *so that*; there is no difference in meaning

   Lina went to the bank so she could get some cash.

   Lina went to the bank so that she could get some cash.

3. so = a common word at the beginning of a statement or question to continue a conversation; not used in academic writing

   Carlos: We went to the beach all day yesterday.

   Maria: So what time did you finally get home last night?

Read the two sentences. Write C (for cause) or R (for result) on each line to show what kind of sentence it is. Then combine them into a compound sentence. Put the cause first, then the connector so, *and then the result. Be sure to put a comma before* so *and add a period at the end of the sentence. The first one has been done for you.*

(NOTE: Sometimes you will need to change nouns to pronouns—for example, *the boy → him; the car → it.*)

1a. ___C___ I was thirsty.

 b. ___R___ I drank three glasses of water.

 I was thirsty, so I drank three glasses of water.

2a. _____ We did not play tennis.

 b. _____ It rained really hard.

 _____

3a. _____ Mrs. Lopez took Ana to the doctor.

 b. _____ Ana was very sick.

 _____

4a. _____ The audience loved the show.

 b. _____ The audience applauded wildly.

 _____

5a. _____ Jonathan did not feel well.

 b. _____ Jonathan did not go to the party.

 _____

6a. _____ I did not buy the DVD.

 b. _____ The DVD was very expensive.

 _____

7a. _____ The plane did not leave on time.

 b. _____ We arrived at our destination late.

 _____

8a. _____ Angela forgot to set her alarm clock.

 b. _____ Angela woke up late.

 _____

For more practice with identifying cause and result, try Unit 5, Activity 3 on the *Great Writing 1* Web site: elt.heinle.com/greatwriting

Study the following pictures. Write what you think is happening based on what you see. Be sure to use the connector so *and the present progressive in your compound sentences. The first one has been done for you.*

1. The woman wants to lose weight, so she is exercising.

2. _____

3. _____

4. _____

_____

_____

_____

_____

_____

_____

_____

5. _____

_____

_____

_____

_____

_____

_____

_____

_____

6. _____

_____

_____

_____

_____

_____

For more practice with compound sentences with *so* and the present progressive, try Unit 5, Activity 4 and Activity 5 on the *Great Writing 1* Web site: elt.heinle.com/greatwriting

Read the following sentences. Some of the sentences are compound sentences, and some are simple sentences. First, identify the type of sentence as S (simple) or C (compound). Then, if the sentence is compound, insert a comma where necessary. The first two have been done for you.

1. __S__ My brother and I went hiking and fishing last weekend.

2. __C__ The motorcycle is in the garage, and the car is in the driveway.

3. _____ Harry and Darlene went to the picnic yesterday and the party last night.

4. _____ I do not know the answer to the question so I will ask the teacher.

5. _____ How many times have you visited Europe and Asia?

6. _____ There are many great places to visit in this city so you cannot see them all in one day.

7. _____ The main agricultural product from the countries in that area of Central Asia is cotton.

8. _____ A noun is a word like *sandwich* and a verb is an action word such as *eat*.

9. _____ Lisana works for a computer company but she does not have a computer engineering degree.

10. _____ Where did you get those beautiful earrings and bracelets?

11. _____ The capital of Sudan is Khartoum and it is the most populated city in the country.

12. _____ The traffic was terrible so Lance missed his plane.

For more practice with reviewing compound sentences and connectors, try Unit 5, Activity 6 and Activity 7 on the *Great Writing 1* Web site: elt.heinle.com/greatwriting

Writer's Note

Using Sentence Variety

Many students who are studying English write short sentences. These sentences usually follow the same pattern: simple subject + simple verb. Good writers do not repeat the same sentence patterns too often. They write some short sentences and some longer sentences. Vary your writing with both simple and compound sentences. Use connectors to show that you can write more advanced sentences in English.

Adverbs

Adverbs are another interesting word group in English. There are several kinds of adverbs in English. Most of them describe verbs.

Grammar and Sentence Structure

Common Adverbs of Manner

In Unit 2 you studied adjectives. These are words that describe nouns.

> Did you see the <u>beautiful</u> baby? The baby is <u>beautiful</u>.

In these sentences, the adjective *beautiful* describes the baby.

Adverbs also describe, but adverbs usually describe verbs.

> Kerry picked up the baby <u>carefully</u>.

> My sister studies <u>hard</u>.

In these examples, the adverbs describe how the action is done. *How* shows manner.

> *How* did Kerry pick up the baby? <u>Carefully</u>.

> *How* does my sister study? <u>Hard</u>.

NOTE: Adverbs of manner usually end in *-ly* and usually follow the verb.

Here is a list of some common adverbs of manner that describe actions:

quickly	easily	nervously	carefully	happily	slowly
suddenly	silently	correctly	fast*	hard*	well*

* These adverbs do not use the *-ly* form.

ACTIVITY 10 Practice with Adverbs

Read each sentence. In the blank, write an adverb that describes the action of the underlined verb. You may choose from the list of common adverbs of manner or use your own adverbs.

1. Joann <u>is studying</u> _____ in the library.

2. She <u>jumped</u> on the bus _____ because it was raining.

3. Mary Ann <u>spoke</u> _____ at the conference.

4. David <u>is doing</u> _____ in this class. He never studies!

5. Norma <u>cried</u> _____ during the movie.

6. Leslie <u>typed</u> the letter _____. I thought she would never finish.

7. Nathalie <u>read</u> the directions _____. She did not want to make a mistake.

8. I had a cold, so I did not <u>play</u> _____ at the soccer game last week.

9. Maria and Faisal <u>passed</u> the test _____ because they <u>studied</u> very

_____ for it.

10. Lawrence <u>opened</u> the door _____ because he was afraid.

ACTIVITY 11 Writing What You See: Describing Actions

Write a paragraph based on observation. Choose a place from which to observe people—for example, a park, a mall, or a cafeteria. You may also use a show on television or an illustration in a magazine. Be sure to choose a situation or place that has several people who are doing different actions. Use the following ideas to help you write a paragraph. The paragraph has been started for you.

- Look at the people. What are they doing?
- Write about an object. What is happening with it?
- Remember to use the connectors *and* and *so* if possible.

_____ There is a lot of action happening right now. _____

_____

_____

_____

_____

_____

_____

_____

_____

_____

_____

_____

Read the following paragraph. There are 10 mistakes in the paragraph: 2 mistakes with compound sentences, 2 mistakes with adverbs, 2 mistakes with verbs, 2 mistakes with adjectives, and 2 mistakes with capitalization. Find and correct the errors. The first one has been done for you.

EXAMPLE PARAGRAPH 55

The Squirrel

A small brown squirrel ^is^ climbing a tree. He looks like a young squirrel. His tail is twitching nervously and his nose is moving quick. I think he is looking for food. Now the squirrel brown is on a long tree branch. He wants to jump to another tree. The squirrel hears something so he looks down. he is coming down from the tree tall. Someone dropped a few pieces of chocolate chip cookie. These pieces lying on the grass. the squirrel is walking toward the food, and he is inspecting it. He is putting it in his mouth. His tail is moving rapid. The little brown squirrel is now eating happily.

⚒ Building Better Sentences

Correct and varied sentence structure is essential to the quality of your writing. For further practice with the sentences and paragraphs in this unit, go to Practice 5 on page 236 in Appendix 1.

ACTIVITY 13 Word Associations

Circle the word or phrase that is most closely related to the word or phrase on the left. If necessary, use a dictionary to check the meaning of words you do not know.

1. to yawn	to use your mouth	to use your ears
2. strong	delicious	powerful
3. thirsty	need water	need food
4. to hear	with your eyes	with your ears
5. a carpet	a rug	a garage
6. to swing	to move back and forth	to stay in one place
7. younger	80 years old	18 years old
8. a mess	very organized	not organized
9. to drop	to select	to fall
10. a piece	a part	a coin
11. to climb	to go near	to go up
12. private	not important	not public
13. to inspect	to wait for	to look at
14. a crowd	a large group	a small group
15. empty	nothing inside	a lot inside

ACTIVITY 14 Using Collocations

Fill in each blank with the word on the left that most naturally completes the phrase on the right. If necessary, use a dictionary to check the meaning of words you do not know.

1. safari / crowd	to be in a _____
2. have / feel	_____ very lucky
3. about / on	to be worried _____

4. dirty / delicious   to wash _____ clothes at the laundry

5. audience / art   to see an _____ exhibit

6. soda / lion   a strong _____

7. machine / cleaner   a vacuum _____

8. trip / family   at the end of the _____

9. room / monkey   an empty _____

10. powerful / nervous   to get _____ about something

ACTIVITY 15 Parts of Speech

Study the following word forms. In the sentences on the right, choose the best word and write it in the blank space. Be sure to use the right form of the verb. If necessary, use a dictionary to check the meaning of words you do not know. (NOTE: The word in bold is the original word that appears in the unit.)

Noun	Verb	Adjective	Sentence Practice
beauty	Ø	**beautiful**	1. Did you see the _____ sunset yesterday?
			2. That painting is a thing of _____.
luck	Ø	**lucky**	3. The _____ lottery winner won $5 million.
			4. It was bad _____ that our team lost the game.
thirst	Ø	**thirsty**	5. If you are _____, drink some iced tea.
			6. Keith is playing tennis. He is probably suffering from _____.
fishing	fish	Ø	7. _____ is a relaxing sport.
			8. We _____ in the lake behind our house.
hiking	hike	Ø	9. Kat _____ every weekend.
			10. Do you like _____?

Noun endings: -ing

Adjective endings: -ful, -y

Original Student Writing

Imagine that you are a TV news reporter. Right now you are at the location of some problem. Describe what is happening around you. Use your imagination!

Now follow these steps for writing. Put a check (✓) next to each step as you complete it. When you finish your paragraph, use the checklist that follows to edit your work. You may want to review What Is a Paragraph? *in Unit 2 on page 39.*

Step 1 _____ In your first sentence, tell where you are and what you are watching.

Step 2 _____ In your next sentence, describe the person, people, or things you see. Use adjectives to give a clear idea to your reader.

Step 3 _____ In the next two to four sentences, describe what the people are doing.

Step 4 _____ Use one or two adverbs in the sentences in Step 3. Remember to place them correctly (usually after the verb).

Step 5 _____ Use *and* or *so* in one of the sentences. Remember to use a comma to separate the two clauses.

Step 6 _____ In the next sentence, write what you think the people are thinking at this moment.

Step 7 _____ In the final sentence, write your opinion about these people.

Step 8 _____ Use at least three of the vocabulary words or phrases presented in Activity 13, Activity 14, and Activity 15. Underline these words and phrases in your paragraph.

✔ Checklist

1. ❑ Make sure every sentence has a subject and a verb.

2. ❑ Be sure that the compound sentences have two subjects and verbs (clauses).

3. ❑ Make sure you use the present progressive verbs correctly.

4. ❑ Make sure every sentence begins with a capital letter.

5. ❑ Make sure every sentence ends with the correct punctuation.

6. ❑ Create a title for your paragraph.

Exchange papers from Activity 16 with a partner. Read your partner's writing. Then use Peer Editing Sheet 5 on page 257 to help you comment on your partner's writing. Be sure to offer positive suggestions and comments that will help your partner improve his or her writing. Consider your partner's comments as you revise your own writing.

Additional Topics for Writing

Here are ten ideas for journal writing. Choose one or more of them to write about. Follow your teacher's directions. (We recommend that you skip a line after each line that you write. This gives your teacher a place to write comments.)

TOPIC 1: Watch several minutes of a television program. Describe what is happening in the show.

TOPIC 2: Describe how your life is now. Include your studies, your living arrangements, and your free time.

TOPIC 3: Imagine that you are a private investigator. Imagine a specific character or person. Write down everything that the person is doing for five minutes.

TOPIC 4: Find a picture in a magazine. Choose a picture of many people who are doing different things. Write a paragraph that describes what each person is doing.

TOPIC 5: Imagine that you are visiting the zoo. What are the animals doing? Write a paragraph that tells what at least five different kinds of animals are doing. Use the connectors *and*, *but*, or *so* to combine short sentences into longer sentences.

TOPIC 6: Imagine that you are in a large city like Tokyo, Toronto, London, Istanbul, or Seoul. Walk around the city and write down the things that you see. What is happening in this large city?

TOPIC 7: Imagine that you are walking down the street, and you see your favorite movie star walk into a café. Follow this person. What is he/she doing?

TOPIC 8: Write a letter to your friend explaining what you are doing in this class. Tell about the assignments that you have and the writing skills that you are practicing.

TOPIC 9: If you have a pet, watch it closely for ten minutes. What is it doing? Where is it going? Is it playing? Jumping? Making noise?

TOPIC 10: Imagine that you are a news reporter for a movie magazine. You are at the Academy Awards presentation. What are the people doing? Name some of the famous actors. (This word means male and female actors.) What are they doing? What are they wearing? What are they saying to their friends? What are they wondering?

Timed Writing

How quickly can you write in English? There are many times when you must write quickly—on a test for example. It is important to feel comfortable during those times. Timed-writing practice can make you feel better about writing quickly in English.

Take out a piece of paper. Then read the writing prompt below this paragraph. Your teacher will give you 5 minutes to brainstorm ideas about the topic. You must write 8 to 10 sentences about this topic. You will have 20 minutes to write these sentences. At the end of the 20 minutes, your teacher will collect your work and return it to you later.

> Describe an exciting (or boring, interesting, etc.) activity that you are doing this year. What is the activity? What are you doing to complete it? Give as many details as possible.

More Writing

For extra writing practice, see the activities in Unit 8 and Appendix 2.

Writing about the Future

GOAL: To learn how to write sentences in the simple future tense

* **Grammar and Sentence Structure:** *Be going to* and *will* for future: statements, questions, and negatives; time words to show the future; articles; using commas in a list

* **Sentence Development:** Complex sentences; answering questions with *because*

Begin with the Simple Future Tense

There are many ways to talk about events that will happen in the future. One way is to use *be going to*. You can use *be going to* when you talk about future plans or when you want to make predictions—or guesses—about the future.

Grammar and Sentence Structure

Be Going To: Statements and Questions

It is easy to make a sentence with *be going to*. Just put the correct form of *be* + *going to* in front of the base form of the verb.

Be Going To: Statements

Verb *study*

I	**am going to study**	we	**are going to study**
you	**are going to study**	you (plural)	**are going to study**
he / she / it	**is going to study**	they	**are going to study**

Study these examples.

Incorrect:	We going to go to the store in a few minutes.
Correct:	We **are** going to go to the store in a few minutes.
Incorrect:	I am going to a sandwich for lunch.
Correct:	I am going to **buy** a sandwich for lunch.
Incorrect:	According to the radio report, the weather going to be severe tonight.
Correct:	According to the radio report, the weather **is** going to be severe tonight.

Be Going To: Questions

Verb _fly_

Am I **going to fly** . . . ?	**Are** we **going to fly** . . . ?
Are you **going to fly** . . . ?	**Are** you (plural) **going to fly** . . . ?
Is he / she / it **going to fly** . . . ?	**Are** they **going to fly** . . . ?

Study these examples.

Incorrect:	Jim and Dave are going to buy a new car?
Correct:	Are Jim and Dave going to buy a new car?
Incorrect:	They going to see a movie this afternoon?
Correct:	Are they going to see a movie this afternoon?
Incorrect:	**Did** you going to visit your parents in December?
Correct:	Are you going to visit your parents in December?

ACTIVITY 1 Making Predictions

Look at each picture. Make a prediction about what will happen. Use the correct form of be going to. _Write complete sentences._

1. _____

   _____

   _____

   _____

2. _____

   _____

   _____

   _____

3. _____

_____

_____

_____

4. _____

_____

_____

_____

5. _____

_____

_____

_____

6. _____

_____

_____

_____

For more practice with identifying the simple future tense and *be going to* statements and questions, try Unit 6, Activity 1 and Activity 2 on the *Great Writing 1* Web site: elt.heinle.com/greatwriting

Avoiding *Gonna* in Writing

Speakers of English often pronounce *going to* as *gonna* in informal speech. However, do not use *gonna* in writing. You must write out the words completely.

Incorrect writing:	I'm gonna buy a new shirt.
Correct writing:	I'm going to buy a new shirt.

Grammar and Sentence Structure

Will: Statements and Questions

Will can also be used to express future time. It is easy to use *will* in a sentence about the future. Just put *will* in front of the base form of the verb.

Will: Statements

Verb *buy*

I	will buy	we	will buy
you	will buy	you (plural)	will buy
he / she / it	will buy	they	will buy

Study these examples.

Incorrect:	She will **goes** to school tomorrow.
Correct:	She will go to school tomorrow.
Incorrect:	They will **are** watch a new movie tonight.
Correct:	They will watch a new movie tonight.
Incorrect:	We will **talking** to the teacher next week.
Correct:	We will talk to the teacher next week.

NOTE: The contraction for *will* is *'ll*.

I will = I'll	we will = we'll
you will = you'll	you (plural) will = you'll
he / she / it will = he'll / she'll / it'll	they will = they'll

Incorrect:	**Shel'l** meet us at the movie theater.
Incorrect:	**Shell'** meet us at the movie theater.
Correct:	She'll meet us at the movie theater.

Will: Questions

Verb *make*

Will I **make . . . ?**   **Will** we **make . . . ?**

Will you **make . . . ?**   **Will** you (plural) **make . . . ?**

Will he / she / it **make . . . ?**   **Will** they **make . . . ?**

Study these examples.

Incorrect:	Rhonda will arrive soon?
Correct:	Will Rhonda arrive soon?
Incorrect:	Will Keith and Jason **plays** soccer this weekend?
Correct:	Will Keith and Jason play soccer this weekend?
Incorrect:	The students take their finals on time this semester?
Correct:	Will the students take their finals on time this semester?

ACTIVITY 2 Writing about the Future

Look at Michael's schedule for next week. Answer the questions using complete sentences. The first one has been done for you. Notice both will *and* be going to *are used.*

Sunday	Monday	Tuesday	Wednesday	Thursday	Friday	Saturday
meet Mom & Dad for lunch	meeting with Mr. Green	take cat to the veterinarian	business report due to Ms. Simms	buy groceries	dinner with Andrea	soccer game 6 p.m.

1. What is Michael going to do on Sunday?

   Michael is going to meet his mom and dad for lunch on Sunday.

2. Who will Michael meet on Monday?

   _____

3. When is he going to have dinner with Andrea?

   _____

4. Where is he going to take his pet?

   _____

5. What will he do on Thursday?

   _____

6. When is he going to play soccer?

_____

7. What will he give to Ms. Simms on Wednesday?

_____

ACTIVITY 3 Practicing with Paragraphs

Review the sentences you wrote about Michael's schedule in Activity 2. Put them in correct time order, starting with Sunday. Write the sentences in paragraph form below. The beginning and the end of the paragraph have been done for you.

EXAMPLE PARAGRAPH 56

Michael's Busy Schedule

Michael is going to be a very busy man next week. First, he is going to meet his mom and dad for lunch on Sunday.

_____

_____

_____

_____

_____

_____

_____

_____

_____

_____

Finally, he is going to play soccer at six o'clock on Saturday. Michael is the busiest man I know!

 For more practice with *will* statements and questions, try Unit 6, Activity 3 on the *Great Writing 1* Web site: elt.heinle.com/greatwriting

Using Time Words and Phrases

Good writers include **time words** and **time phrases** in their writing. Time words and phrases give important information about *when* something happens.

Grammar and Sentence Structure

Time Words and Phrases

Study this list of time words and phrases. Do you know the meanings of all of them?

first	tomorrow	in a minute	next week
next	next Saturday	later	next year
finally	next January	then	next time
after that	before that		

Time words usually occur at the beginning or the end of a sentence. However, they can sometimes occur in the middle of a sentence. Look at these examples of time words and phrases at the beginning and at the end of sentences.

We are going to go to the movies <u>on Saturday</u>.

<u>On Saturday,</u> we are going to go to the movies.

The airline will produce a new kind of jet <u>in the next few months</u>.

<u>In the next few months,</u> the airline will produce a new kind of jet.

We are going to paint the kitchen <u>first</u>.

<u>First,</u> we are going to paint the kitchen.

A comma usually follows the time words and phrases at the beginning of a sentence.

NOTE: *Then* is not followed by a comma.

ACTIVITY 4 Practicing with Time Words

Fill in the blanks with these time words: then, next, first, after, Sunday, finally. *One word can be used twice. Add commas where necessary.*

EXAMPLE PARAGRAPH 57

A Reunion to Remember

This year's family reunion will be special because we are going to celebrate my Aunt Laura's ninety-eighth birthday. (**1.**) _____ everyone in our family will travel to my aunt's town for the weekend. The (**2.**) _____ night, we are going to meet at Aunt Laura's house and eat a big dinner. (**3.**) _____ dinner, we are going to bring out a big birthday cake. (4.) _____ we will sing to her and give her presents. She is going to love it! The

(5.) _____ day, the whole family will meet in the city park for a big picnic. There will

be food, games, and music for everyone. Aunt Laura will give a nice speech to the family, too. On

(6.) _____ everyone will go to lunch with Aunt Laura. (7.) _____ our

special celebration will be over, and everyone will return home dreaming about next year's reunion.

For more practice with time words and using commas with time words, try Unit 6, Activity 4 and Activity 5
on the *Great Writing 1* Web site: elt.heinle.com/greatwriting

ACTIVITY 5 Responding to a Reading Passage

*Read the paragraph and underline the 10 simple future tense verbs. (Hint: Two of them might be difficult
to find.) Then answer the questions that follow.*

Carmen's Fifteenth Birthday

Next week, Carmen Viera is going to be 15 years old, and her family has plans for a special

celebration for her. On her birthday, Carmen is going to wear a beautiful white **gown**. First, she is

going to go to church with her family and friends. After church is over, they will go to an **elegant**

ballroom. Then they are going to have a party called a *quince*. When Carmen arrives, she will

perform some formal dances with her friends. After that, everyone is going to dance, eat, and

celebrate. Carmen can **hardly** wait. She knows that she will always remember her special day.

a gown: a long, formal dress
elegant: graceful; refined
a ballroom: a large room where formal parties
  are held

a quince: the Spanish word for fifteen; a traditional Latin
  birthday party that celebrates when a girl becomes a woman
hardly: almost not; with difficulty (a negative word)

1. How old is Carmen going to be next week?

_____

2. What is Carmen going to wear on her birthday?

_____

3. What is the first thing she is going to do on her birthday?

_____

4. Where are they going to hold her *quince* party?

_____

5. What are Carmen and her friends going to do at the party?

_____

Be Going To and Will with Negatives

You know how to use *be going to* and *will* to talk about events that happen in the future. You learned how to make affirmative statements and how to ask questions about the future. It is also important to know how to talk about things that are not going to happen in the future.

Grammar and Sentence Structure

Be Going To and Will: Negative

To make *be going to* negative, write the word *not* between the *be* verb and *going to*. Study this chart of *be going to* with the negative *not*.

I	**am <u>not</u> going to study**	we	**are <u>not</u> going to study**
you	**are <u>not</u> going to study**	you (plural)	**are <u>not</u> going to study**
he / she / it	**is <u>not</u> going to study**	they	**are <u>not</u> going to study**

NOTE: You can make contractions with these negative verbs.

are not = aren't   is not = isn't

Study these examples.

Incorrect:	I am going to **not** talk.
Correct:	I am (I'm) not going to talk.
Incorrect:	Jane not going to sing on Sunday.
Correct:	Jane **is** not (isn't) going to sing on Sunday.
Incorrect:	Brett and Erica **no** going to play soccer.
Correct:	Brett and Erica are not (aren't) going to play soccer.

To make *will* negative, write the word *not* after it. Study this chart of *will* with the negative *not*.

I	will **not** write	we	will **not** write
you	will **not** write	you (plural)	will **not** write
he / she / it	will **not** write	they	will **not** write

NOTE: You can make a contraction with *will* and *not*.

will not = won't

Study these examples.

Incorrect:	They will not **to** come to the party.
Correct:	They will not (won't) come to the party.
Incorrect:	The president not make a speech on television tonight.
Correct:	The president will not (won't) make a speech on television tonight.
Incorrect:	My company will **don't** give me a raise this year.
Correct:	My company will not (won't) give me a raise this year.

ACTIVITY 6 Writing Original Sentences

Think of something important or special that you are going to do in the future. Answer these questions.

1. What is one important thing that you are going to do in your life?

   _____

   _____

2. How long will it take to do it?

   _____

3. What are you going to do to accomplish this goal? (Write at least three things.)

   _____

   _____

   _____

   _____

4. How will you feel when you accomplish this goal? Why?

   _____

   _____

Complex Sentences

In Unit 5, you learned that sentence variety is important. Good writers write both **simple** and **compound sentences**. There is another way to add variety to your sentence writing: **complex sentences**.

Sentence Development

Sentence Variety: Complex Sentences

One way to combine two sentences into one is to use a connecting word that is part of the sentence. Some of these connecting words are *after*, *before*, *because*, *if*, *although*, *since*, and *when*. Unlike the connectors in compound sentences (*and*, *but*, *so*), the connecting words in complex sentences are a necessary part of one of the sentences (clauses). This type of sentence is called a **complex sentence**. Look at these examples:

Compound sentence: Joe played tennis, and Vicky watched TV.

This sentence has three parts: sentence + the connector *and* + sentence.

| Joe played tennis, | + | and | + | Vicky watched TV. |

Complex sentence: Joe played tennis after Vicky watched TV.

This sentence has two parts: one simple sentence + one sentence that begins with the connecting word *after*.

| Joe played tennis | + | after Vicky watched TV. |

The word *after* is not a part by itself. This word is part of the idea of *when* Vicky watched TV. The group of words with the connecting word must always be connected to another sentence. Otherwise, it is a *fragment*. (See Unit 1, page 17, for information on fragments.)

Here are a few more examples of complex sentences.

| My mom is going to make dinner | when my dad gets home. |

| Alana is going to get a full-time job | after she graduates. |

| As soon as we get paid | , | we are going to buy some new clothes. |

| Because it is cold outside | , | they are going to wear jackets. |

Commas in Complex Sentences

When a complex sentence begins with a clause that contains a connecting word, put a comma at the end of the clause.

CONNECTING WORD CLAUSE

Comma: After she ate dinner, she called her friend.

CONNECTING WORD CLAUSE

No comma: She called her friend after she ate dinner.

*For more information on complex sentences, read about subordinating conjunctions in the Brief Writer's Handbook, page 227.

Writer's Note

Verbs in Complex Sentences

Here is a rule for writing complex sentences about the *future*: Use the *simple present tense* in the clause with the time word. Use the *simple future tense* in the other clause. Do not use the simple future tense in both clauses.

Incorrect: When the rain **will** stop, I am going to rake the leaves.

Correct: When the rain stops, I am going to rake the leaves.

Incorrect: When Flight 873 **will** arrive in Paris, the police will arrest a passenger on the plane.

Correct: When Flight 873 arrives in Paris, the police will arrest a passenger on the plane.

ACTIVITY 7 Identifying Sentence Types

Read the following sentences. Some of the sentences are simple, some are compound, and some are complex. First, identify the type of sentence as S (simple), CD (compound), or CX (complex). If the sentence is compound or complex, insert a comma if necessary. The first three have been done for you.

1. ___S___ I am going to go scuba diving next weekend.

2. ___CD___ My father is going to retire next year, but my mother is going to continue working.

3. ___CX___ After he came home from the beach, Gerardo took a shower.

4. _____ Irene is going to call you when she gets home from work.

5. _____ We are going to go to the mall and the beach next Sunday.

6. _____ Ariel is going to go to college next year but her brother is going to get a job.

7. _____ When the game is over we are going to eat at Harvey's Grill.

8. _____ How often do you work out at the gym?

9. _____ Leslie and Serena are sisters but they do not get along very well.

10. _____ Billy and his friends went to the hockey game and cheered for their team.

11. _____ If the pilot gets sick during a flight the copilot takes over.

12. _____ The copilot plays an important role in the success of a flight.

 For more practice with identifying sentence types, try Unit 6, Activity 6 on the *Great Writing 1* Web site: elt.heinle.com/greatwriting

Answer the following questions. Use time words in your answer. If the question includes a time word, write a complex sentence for your answer. You can use the connecting words in the Sentence Variety section on page 149. The first one has been done for you.

1. What are you going to do after you graduate?

   <u>After I graduate, I am going to look for a job.</u>

2. What are you going to do as soon as you finish this activity?

   _____

3. What are you not going to do before you go to bed tonight?

   _____

4. When are you going to do your homework?

   _____

5. When are you going to eat dinner?

   _____

6. What are you going to do after you eat dinner?

   _____

Articles *A*, *An*, and *The*

A, *an*, and *the* are three of the shortest words in English, but they are also three of the most important words. These words are called **articles**. They are very important in correct writing and speaking. In this section, you are going to learn about the uses of these three words.

Grammar and Sentence Structure

Using Articles in a Sentence

Good writers always use articles in the correct places. There are many rules for using articles in English.

A/An—*Indefinite Articles*

In Unit 3, you learned to use *a/an* when you have a singular count noun and are talking about something in general. Use *a* if the next word begins with a consonant sound. Use *an* if the next word begins with a vowel sound.

   I bought <u>a</u> sweater.

   Wendy wants <u>an</u> ice cream cone.

Remember: there are some exceptions to the consonant/vowel rule. If the beginning letter *h* is silent (as in *honor*), use *an* before it. If the beginning letter *u* sounds like the word *you* (as in *university*), use *a* before it. Remember to pay attention to the <u>sound</u> of the beginning of the word, not the letter that it begins with.

Incorrect:	Meet me at the library in **a** hour.
Correct:	Meet me at the library in an hour.
Incorrect:	John bought **an** unique gift for his mother.
Correct:	John bought a unique gift for his mother.
Incorrect:	Does your last name begin with **a** *e* or **a** *n*?
Correct:	Does your last name begin with an *e* or an *n*?

The—*Definite Article*

The can be used with both singular and plural count and non-count* nouns. Here are some basic rules for using *the*.

1. Use *the* for the second (and subsequent) time you talk about something.

   I bought a sweater and a coat yesterday.

   The sweater is made of wool, but the coat is made of leather.

2. Use *the* when the speaker and the listener both know about or are familiar with the subject.

   Are you going to <u>the bank</u> this afternoon?

3. Use *the* when the noun you are referring to is unique—there is only one.

   <u>The Sun</u> and <u>the Earth</u> are both in <u>the Milky Way</u> galaxy.

   <u>The Eiffel Tower</u> is a beautiful monument.

(See the Brief Writer's Handbook, pages 222–223, for a more complete list of when to use the article *the*.)

*Non-count nouns are nouns that do not use a plural form such as *money, butter, homework, gold,* and *honesty*.

Examples:	Honesty is important. (not *the honesty*)
	When people discuss politics, they often disagree. (not *the politics*)

(See the Brief Writer's Handbook, page 223, for a short list of common non-count nouns.)

Article Use Chart

Study this chart to help you remember the basic rules for using articles:

When Your Meaning Is:	Singular Count Nouns*	Plural Count Nouns	Non-count Nouns
General	*a/an*	Ø**	Ø
Specific	*the*	*the*	*the*

*Count nouns are nouns that have a plural form:

book—books   woman—women   child—children   house—houses

**Ø means do not use an article.

Writer's Note

Singular Count Nouns and Modifiers

A singular count noun (*car, woman*) can never stand on its own in a sentence. An article (*a, an, the*), a possessive adjective (*my, your, his*), or a quantifier (*one, another, some*) *must* come before it. (See the Brief Writer's Handbook, page 224, for more examples of possessive adjectives and quantifiers.)

Look at the following sentences.

Incorrect: April owns cat.

Correct: April owns <u>a</u> cat. (article)

Incorrect: I am reading book.

Correct: I am reading <u>my</u> book. (possessive adjective)

Incorrect: Give me spoon. This one is dirty.

Correct: Give me <u>another</u> spoon. This one is dirty. (quantifier)

Read the paragraph. Write a, an, *or the* in the blanks.

A World Traveler

Robert likes to travel a lot, and next year he is going to go on (**1.**) _____ excellent trip.

(**2.**) _____ trip is going to be to Egypt and New Zealand. He wants to meet a lot of new people

and try interesting food. While he is in Egypt, he is going to see (**3.**) _____ Great Pyramids

at Giza and (**4.**) _____ Sphinx of Cheops. He wants to take (**5.**) _____ cruise down

(**6.**) _____ Nile River, but it is probably going to be too expensive. After he visits Egypt, he will

fly to New Zealand to visit (**7.**) _____ cousin who lives there. His cousin's name is Thomas.

Robert and Thomas are going to hike along the coast of New Zealand for a few weeks. They

want to see (**8.**) _____ tuatara. Tuataras are lizards from (**9.**) _____ ancient reptile family.

Because tuataras are **nocturnal**, it is going to be difficult to see them. Finally, they will take

(**10.**) _____ bike trip on (**11.**) _____ North Island. It is going to be a fun trip.

nocturnal: active at night

Create complete sentences and questions from the prompts below. Remember to add the correct article (a, an, the) *to the sentences where necessary. Use the correct verb tense, punctuation, and capitalization. The first one has been done for you.*

1. robert / go (negative) / to / beach / tomorrow

   <u>Robert is not going to go to the beach tomorrow.</u>

2. laura's parents / visit / eiffel tower / in paris / last year

   _____

3. we / have / grammar test / next week (question)

   _____

4. weather / be / very / nice / for / picnic / last Saturday

   _____

5. carol / bob / see / owl / in / tree / in their backyard / last night / and

   _____

6. you / go / movies / every friday night (question)

   _____

7. computer / not work / anymore

   _____

8. I / bring / apple / sandwich / for lunch yesterday / and

   _____

9. after nicholas / graduate last week / his sister / give him / expensive gift

   _____

10. my dad / buy / me / bike / for / my last birthday / but / I / want / puppy

    _____

For more practice with definite and indefinite articles, try Unit 6, Activity 7 on the *Great Writing 1* Web site: elt.heinle.com/greatwriting

Questions and Answers: Structures with *Because*

You have learned that one way to write complex sentences is with words such as *after*, *before*, *when*, and *if*. In this section, you are going to learn how to write complex sentences with the connector *because*.

Sentence Development

Answering Questions with *Because*

How would you answer this question: *Why did you decide to study English?*
One popular way to answer a *why* question is to use the word *because* in the answer.

I am studying English <u>because</u> I wanted to learn a second language.

I am studying English <u>because</u> I want to study in an English-speaking country.

I am studying English <u>because</u> I like the way it sounds.

Notice how these sentences are organized. The first part of each sentence contains part of the question. It is then followed by *because*. The word *because* is followed by the reason (answer). Each example sentence has two clauses. (Remember: a clause has a subject and a verb.) In formal writing, a clause with *because* must be part of a complex sentence.

Fragments

If your sentence has *because* and one subject and verb only, the sentence is incorrect—it is a fragment. Fragments are not correct in formal writing. Study the following sentences.

Incorrect: We did not go to the beach. Because it was raining.
                       (FRAGMENT)

Correct: We did not go to the beach because it was raining.
           (COMPLEX SENTENCE)

Incorrect: Megan is going to the disco. Because she likes to dance.
                        (FRAGMENT)

Correct: Megan is going to the disco because she likes to dance.
         (COMPLEX SENTENCE)

NOTE: *Because* can also be used at the beginning of a sentence. When it is, you must put a comma at the end of the clause. This is a complex sentence.

Incorrect: Because his brother broke the computer Alan got angry.

Correct: Because his brother broke the computer, Alan got angry.

(See Unit 1, page 17, for more information on fragments.)

ACTIVITY 11 Sentence or Fragment?

Read each group of words. If it is a fragment, write F on the line. If it is a complete sentence, write S on the line and add correct capitalization and punctuation. The first two have been done for you.

1. __S__ ~~dante~~ D͟ante passed the test because he studied hard.

2. __F__ because the test has 50 questions

3. _____ because it was raining we did not go to the beach

4. _____ because everyone had a wonderful time at the party

5. _____ she arrived late because her car broke down

6. _____ because he forgot about his appointment

7. _____ because I live in new york I go to the theater on broadway often

8. _____ because some committee members did not attend the conference

9. _____ the computers were down today because a storm knocked out the power

10. _____ we are going to postpone the meeting because the managers are out of the office

ACTIVITY 12 Using *Because* to Answer a Question

Answer the following questions using a complex sentence with because. *Write complete sentences. The first one has been done for you.*

1. Why are you studying English?

   I am studying English because I want to enter Cornell University next year.

2. Why is soccer a popular sport?

   _____

3. Why is fast food popular in the United States?

   _____

4. Why do you like your hobby?

   _____

5. Why do some people like to drive fast?

   _____

6. Why are you using this book?

   _____

7. Why do you write letters to your family?

_____

8. Why do some people skip breakfast in the morning?

_____

9. Why do children learn to print before they learn cursive writing?

_____

10. Why is hip-hop music popular?

_____

✎ Writer's Note

Using Commas between Words in a List

The comma (,) is one of the most important marks of punctuation in English sentences. Commas help to make the meaning of sentences clear.

Sometimes good writers write sentences that contain a list of three or more things. Here are some examples.

ITEM 1   ITEM 2   ITEM 3   ITEM 4
Jennifer will visit London, Paris, Rome, and Prague next year. (list of nouns)

ITEM 1 ITEM 2   ITEM 3
Andrea is going to grow pink, yellow, and white roses in her garden. (list of adjectives)

You must put a comma after each item in the list except the last one. In addition, try to keep the words the same part of speech. For example, if you have three words, all three words should be nouns (or verbs or adjectives). The point is not to mix up the kinds of words. (See the Brief Writer's Handbook, page 228, for more comma rules.)

ACTIVITY 13 Practicing Comma Rules

For each item, combine the sentences into one sentence. Remember the comma rules that you have practiced for compound sentences, complex sentences, and lists. You may have to change or delete some words. The first one has been done for you.

1. I bought a shirt and a skirt at the mall. I got a winter coat.

   <u>I bought a shirt, a skirt, and a winter coat at the mall.</u>

2. Michael likes to play soccer. He likes to play hockey and football.

_____

_____

_____

3. My friend Rick is angry with me. My friends Susan and Greg are angry with me.

_____

_____

_____

4. John wants to go to the movies. Robert and Theo want to go, too.

_____

_____

_____

5. I am going to bring sunglasses and a towel to the beach tomorrow. I am also going to bring a cold drink and a book.

_____

_____

_____

6. At the dance, we ate food. We danced, and we played games.

_____

_____

_____

7. In Moscow, Candice is going to visit the Kremlin and St. Basil's Cathedral. She is going to go to Gorky Park.

_____

_____

_____

8. Ron and Harry rode the Ferris wheel at the fair. Elizabeth rode the Ferris wheel.

_____

_____

_____

Read the following paragraph. There are 10 errors in the paragraph. Find and correct them. If you need help finding the errors, look at the numbers in parentheses on the left side of the paragraph. This number tells you how many errors are in each line. The first one has been done for you.

EXAMPLE PARAGRAPH 60

My Winter Vacation

(1)   My winter vacation is going to be wonderful because I am going to go to ~~q~~uebec. *Q*

(1) I am going to go with my best friend. We going to spend two weeks there, and it is going

(2) to be a wonderful time. I have the aunt who lives there, and she going to show us all the

(3) sights beautiful. We do not speak french very well so we are a little bit nervous. After I

(3) arrive in Canada I am going to buy a lot of souvenirs for my parents brother and friends.

I cannot wait for my vacation to begin!

🔨 Building Better Sentences

Correct and varied sentence structure is essential to the quality of your writing. For further practice with the sentences and paragraphs in this unit, go to Practice 6 on pages 236–237 in Appendix 1.

ACTIVITY 15 Word Associations

Circle the word or phrase that is most closely related to the word or phrase on the left. If necessary, use a dictionary to check the meaning of words you do not know.

1. a reunion	a gathering of friends		a gathering of animals
2. presents	attendance		gifts
3. a speech	written communication		verbal communication
4. to celebrate	to have fun		to be quiet
5. formal	most common		most proper
6. to forget	to not graduate		to not remember
7. hardly	very difficult		almost not at all
8. angry	strong negative emotion		strong positive emotion
9. to hike	to walk		to run
10. honesty	lies		truth
11. few	not near		not many
12. ancient	very new		very old
13. nocturnal	awake during the day		awake at night
14. a vacation	a time for work		a time for fun
15. a cousin	your uncle's child		your mother's child

ACTIVITY 16 Using Collocations

Fill in each blank with the word on the left that most naturally completes the phrase on the right. If necessary, use a dictionary to check the meaning of words you do not know.

1. building / vacation	an ancient _____
2. about / for	to forget _____ something
3. between / along	to drive _____ the coast of Nova Scotia
4. sight / animal	a nocturnal _____
5. honest / unique	a(n) _____ experience

6.	ballroom / speech	an informative _____	
7.	formal / honest	this is a(n) _____ event	
8.	sights / souvenirs	to visit all the _____	
9.	honest / angry	to get _____	
10.	speech / cruise	to attend a _____	

ACTIVITY 17 Parts of Speech

Study the following word forms. In the sentences on the right, choose the best word and write it in the blank space. Be sure to use the correct form of the verb. If necessary, use a dictionary to check the meaning of words you do not know. (NOTE: The word in bold is the original word that appears in the unit.)

Noun	Verb	Adjective	Sentence Practice
anger	anger	**angry**	1. She is going to be _____ when I tell her the news.
			2. The children _____ their mother yesterday.
honesty	Ø	honest	3. Please give me an _____ answer.
			4. _____ is the best policy.
nerve/nervou<u>ness</u>	Ø	**nervous**	5. Bill was _____ about taking the exam.
			6. I can see the _____ in her expression.
formal<u>ity</u>	formal<u>ize</u>	**formal**	7. The dance next week is going to be _____.
			8. Meeting the new university president is only a _____.
unique<u>ness</u>	Ø	**unique**	9. The _____ of the Hungarian language makes it difficult to learn.
			10. Charmaine's style of dress is _____.

Noun endings: -y, -ness, -ity

Verb endings: -ize

Adjective endings: -y

Original Student Writing

Reread the paragraph on Carmen Viera in Activity 5 on page 146. Then review your answers to Activity 6 on page 148. Use the information from Activity 6 to write about an event that is going to happen to you in the future.

Then follow these steps for writing. Put a check (✓) next to each step as you complete it. When you finish your paragraph, use the checklist that follows to edit your work. You may want to review What Is a Paragraph? *in Unit 2 on page 39.*

Step 1 _____ In your first sentence, tell who you are and what you are going to do in the future.

Step 2 _____ In the next two sentences, give more details to describe what you are going to do.

Step 3 _____ In the next four or five sentences, describe how you are going to achieve this goal.

Step 4 _____ In the last sentence, tell why it is important for you to achieve this goal. (Use the word *because* in the final sentence.)

Step 5 _____ Try to use time words, such as *after* and *as soon as,* in some of your sentences in Step 3.

Step 6 _____ Try to include a list of three or more items in one of the sentences in Step 3. Remember the comma rule!

Step 7 _____ Write at least one compound and one complex sentence in your paragraph.

Step 8 _____ Use at least three of the vocabulary words or phrases presented in Activity 15, Activity 16, and Activity 17. Underline these words and phrases in your paragraph.

✓ Checklist

1. ❏ Make sure that you use *be going to* or *will* when you talk about the future.

2. ❏ Make sure that you use articles correctly in your sentences.

3. ❏ Make sure that you use commas correctly.

4. ❏ Make sure every sentence has a subject and a verb—no fragments!

5. ❏ Create a title for your paragraph.

Exchange papers from Activity 18 with a partner. Read your partner's writing. Then use Peer Editing Sheet 6 on page 259 to help you comment on your partner's writing. Be sure to offer positive suggestions and comments that will help your partner improve his or her writing. Consider your partner's comments as you revise your own writing.

Additional Topics for Writing

Here are ten ideas for journal writing. Choose one or more of them to write about. Follow your teacher's directions. (We recommend that you skip a line after each line that you write. This gives your teacher a place to write comments.)

TOPIC 1: Write about something that you plan to do in the next two weeks. Include the people who are going to be with you, where you are going to be, and why you are going to do this.

TOPIC 2: Write about something that you plan to do in the next six months. Be sure to include where this activity is going to happen, who is going to be with you, and why you chose this activity.

TOPIC 3: Choose a current topic in the news. Read about it. Then write about what you think will happen and tell why.

TOPIC 4: Write about one of your goals. Include what the goal is, why this goal is important to you, and how long it is going to take to achieve.

TOPIC 5: Write about what you are going to do before you return home today. Make a list: Who are you going to be with? Are you going to do this thing for work, school, or pleasure? How long is it going to take you to complete these things?

TOPIC 6: Describe what your wedding will be like. How big will the wedding party be? Who will be there? Where will it happen?

TOPIC 7: Describe the job you want to have when you finish school. What kind of job is it? What are your responsibilities going to be in this job? Are you going to work for a company or for yourself? How much money are you going to earn in this job?

TOPIC 8: Write about what you plan to study (your major) in college. Why did you choose this subject? What classes are going to be easy for you, and what classes are going to be difficult? How long is it going to take you to get your degree?

TOPIC 9: Describe what life is going to be like in the year 2050. What new things are going to be available? How is life going to be better than it is now? How is life going to be worse than it is now?

TOPIC 10: Write about the future of space travel. What planets are humans going to visit? What things are going to be discovered in space?

Timed Writing

How quickly can you write in English? There are many times when you must write quickly—on a test for example. It is important to feel comfortable during those times. Timed-writing practice can make you feel better about writing quickly in English.

Take out a piece of paper. Then read the writing prompt below this paragraph. Your teacher will give you 5 minutes to brainstorm ideas about the topic. You must write 8 to 10 sentences about this topic. You will have 20 minutes to write these sentences. At the end of the 20 minutes, your teacher will collect your work and return it to you later.

> Describe something that you plan to do next year. Be sure to include who is going to be with you, where it will happen, and why you are going to do this.

More Writing

For extra writing practice, see the activities in Unit 8 and Appendix 2.

Writing Sentences with Adjective Clauses and Place Phrases

GOAL: To learn how to write sentences with adjective clauses and place phrases

* **Grammar and Sentence Structure:** Place phrases; modals

* **Sentence Development:** Sentences with adjective clauses

Writing with Adjective Clauses

It is important that the sentences in a paragraph have variety. If they do not, the paragraph can be boring to read. You have already learned some things about sentence variety. You learned about compound sentences in Units 3–5 and complex sentences in Unit 6. In this unit, you will learn about sentences with **adjective clauses**.

Recognizing Sentence Variety

Each of the following paragraphs contains similar information about tennis terms. However, one of the paragraphs sounds better than the other two. Read the three paragraphs. Which one do you think is the best? Why?

EXAMPLE PARAGRAPH 61A

Tennis Terms

Tennis has many special terms. Most people do not know what these terms mean. One special word is *love*. In tennis, *love* means "nothing" or "zero." Another word is *deuce*. *Deuce* is a special term. *Deuce* means the score is tied at three points for each player. Another term is *volley*. A volley is a shot. Usually, a player runs to the net to try to end the point. The player hits the ball before it touches the ground. *Love*, *deuce*, and *volley* are special words. (86 words, 12 sentences)

Tennis Terms

Tennis has many special terms. Tennis players understand these terms. Some people do not play tennis. Most of these people do not have any idea about the meaning of these terms. *Love* has a special meaning in tennis. For example, in tennis, *love* means "nothing" or "zero." Another word is *deuce*. When tennis players use this word, it means each player has three points. In other words, *deuce* means the score is tied at three points for each player. Another term is *volley*. A volley is a shot. The player hits this shot before the ball touches the ground. Usually, a player runs to the net to try to end the point. The player hits the ball before it touches the ground. *Love, deuce,* and *volley* are special words. All tennis players certainly know these words. (136 words, 16 sentences)

Tennis Terms

Tennis has many special terms that tennis players know. Most people who do not play tennis do not understand the meaning of these terms. For example, one special word is *love*. In tennis, love means "nothing" or "zero." Another word that tennis players use is *deuce*. *Deuce* is a special term that means each player has three points. In other words, *deuce* means the score is tied at three points for each player. Another term that is used by tennis players is *volley*. A volley is a shot that the player hits before the ball touches the ground. Usually, a player runs to the net to try to end the point. The player hits the ball before it touches the ground. *Love, deuce,* and *volley* are special words that all tennis players certainly know. (134 words, 12 sentences)

Evaluating the Paragraphs

Here are one teacher's comments about these three example paragraphs.

Example 1: <u>Many sentences are short and choppy. The information doesn't flow smoothly or connect well. Here are some poor sentences from Example 1:</u>

Deuce is a special term.

Another term is *volley*.

A volley is a shot.

Example 2: <u>This paragraph is better. For example, this complex sentence is an improvement.</u>

When tennis players use this word, it means each player has three points.

<u>However, there are still a few short, choppy sentences. Some information is repeated in different sentences. Here are some poor sentences from Example 2:</u>

Tennis has many special terms. Tennis players understand these terms.

Another term is *volley*. A volley is a shot.

Example 3: <u>Did you think this is the best paragraph? Well, it is. The sentence combinations and variety are much better. Here are some good sentences from Example 3:</u>

Deuce is a special term that means each player has three points.

Another term that is used by tennis players is *volley*.

A volley is a shot that the player hits before the ball touches the ground.

Sentence Development
Combining Sentences with Adjective Clauses: *Who* and *That*

One way to combine two short sentences into a longer or better sentence is through the use of an adjective clause.

Reviewing Clauses

A clause is *any* group of words that includes a subject and a verb. (A sentence, for example, is a clause.) An adjective clause describes a noun. An adjective clause often begins with *who* or *that*.

NOTE: Use *who* in clauses that describe people. Use *that* in clauses that describe things.

Sentences with Adjective Clauses

Study these examples. Notice how the adjective clause comes *directly after* the noun it describes.

Two sentences:	Joe bought a book. The book is very easy to read.
One sentence:	Joe bought a book <u>that is very easy to read</u>.
	ADJECTIVE CLAUSE

Two sentences:	The teacher is Mrs. Habib. She cares about her students.
One sentence:	The teacher <u>who cares about her students</u> is Mrs. Habib.
	ADJECTIVE CLAUSE

Write that *or* who *on the lines.*

An Old Family Photo

This is an old photo of my family. In fact, this is a photo (**1.**) _____ was taken about sixty years ago. I remember the old sofa (**2.**) _____ was in my parents' living room. The two women (**3.**) _____ are sitting on the sofa are my mother and my grandmother. The woman (**4.**) _____ has curly hair is my grandmother. The woman (**5.**) _____ has long hair is my mother. The little boy (**6.**) _____ is on the sofa is Uncle Bob. The sofa in the picture is really old. In fact, this is the sofa (**7.**) _____ my grandmother received from her mother years before. The man (**8.**) _____ is standing behind my grandmother is my grandfather. The two men (**9.**) _____ are to the right of my grandfather are my father and Uncle Sam. The cat (**10.**) _____ you see next to the sofa was my mother's pet. The name (**11.**) _____ my mother gave her cat was Butterball because it was such a big, fat cat. This picture is so important to me because all of the people that I love the most are in it. **Certainly** this is a picture (**12.**) _____ I will **cherish** for many more years.

certainly: without a doubt; definitely   **cherish:** to treat with tenderness

 For more practice with using *who* or *that*, try Unit 7, Activity 1 and Activity 2 on the *Great Writing 1* Web site: elt.heinle.com/greatwriting

Writer's Note

Using *Who* or *That* for *People*

Remember that adjective clauses that begin with *who* describe <u>people</u> only. Adjective clauses that begin with *that* can be for <u>people</u> or <u>things</u>. However, it is preferable to use *who* when you are describing people.

Incorrect:	I bought a fish **who** is orange and white.
Correct:	I bought a fish that is orange and white.
Acceptable:	Many people that watch basketball on TV also watch football.
Preferable:	Many people who watch basketball on TV also watch football.

ACTIVITY 2 Adjective Clauses at the End of a Sentence

In each item, combine the two sentences into one by using an adjective clause. Add the second sentence to the end of the first one, using who *or* that. *The first one has been done for you.*

1. The hula hoop is a toy. The hula hoop became popular in the 1960s.

   The hula hoop is a toy that became popular in the 1960s.

2. New Hampshire is a small state. New Hampshire is in the northeastern part of the United States.

   _____

   _____

3. Romansch is a language. Romansch comes from Latin.

   _____

   _____

4. Bolivia is a South American country. Bolivia does not have a coastline.

   _____

   _____

5. Nasi lemak is a Malaysian dish. Nasi lemak uses white rice and coconut milk.

   _____

   _____

6. Dante Alighieri was an Italian writer. Dante Alighieri wrote *The Divine Comedy*.

   _____

   _____

7. A meerkat is a rodent. It is a native of Africa.

_____

_____

8. The *Titanic* was a ship. It sank in the North Atlantic Ocean.

_____

_____

9. A coach is a person. A coach trains athletes to perform well in sports.

_____

_____

10. The Burj Al Arab is a famous building. The building is on the coast of Dubai.

_____

_____

ACTIVITY 3 Sentence Combining: Adjective Clauses in the Middle of a Sentence

In each item, combine the two sentences into one by using an adjective clause. Use the second piece of information in the middle of your new sentence. **You will need to delete words from the second sentence.** *The first one has been done for you.*

1. The food is called hummus. I like this food the best.

   The food that I like the best is called hummus.

2. The movie was *Steel Magnolias*. We saw this movie on television last night.

   _____

3. The day was October 11. We arrived in Texas on this day.

   _____

4. The number was incorrect. Paul gave me this number.

   _____

5. The story was extremely interesting. Samir told this story.

   _____

6. The homework assignment was difficult. The grammar teacher gave us the homework assignment.

   _____

7. The man is my friend. The man is standing on the street corner.

_____

8. The food got cold. We bought the food for dinner.

_____

9. The police officer was very angry. The police officer gave me a speeding ticket.

_____

10. The play is very popular in London. We are going to see this play tonight.

_____

ACTIVITY 4 Identifying Adjective Clauses in a Paragraph

Read the paragraph and underline the three sentences that have adjective clauses.

EXAMPLE PARAGRAPH 63

A Possible Problem with the Schools

The school **district** in our city has a problem. The teachers who work in the city's schools say they might **go on strike**. The problem is money. The teachers want to go on strike because they get **salaries** that are very low. They say the salaries are not fair, so they want the school **officials** to **raise** teachers' salaries. There will be an emergency meeting of the school board this evening, and the public is invited. The teachers hope the people who attend the meeting will agree with them about the low salaries. Will the teachers go on strike? We are going to learn the answer to this question at tonight's meeting.

a district: an official area or community
go on strike: to protest by not working
salary: money that a person earns

an official: a director, a leader
raise: to make higher

ACTIVITY 5 Examining Adjective Clauses

Look at the three sentences that you underlined in Activity 4. Copy each of them below. Then write the short sentences that were combined to make the longer sentence.

Sentence 1: _____

    a. _____

    b. _____

Sentence 2: _____

     a. _____

     b. _____

     c. _____

Sentence 3: _____

     a. _____

     b. _____

For more practice with identifying adjective clauses, try Unit 7, Activity 3 on the *Great Writing 1* Web site: elt.heinle.com/greatwriting

ACTIVITY 6 Sentence Combining: Adjective Clauses

Each paragraph is missing a sentence. Create the missing sentence from the sentences below the paragraph. Use all the ideas but not necessarily all the words. Your new sentence should have an adjective clause and be a good supporting sentence. Write your new sentence on the lines in the paragraph.

EXAMPLE PARAGRAPH 64

Some English Spelling Problems

Some English words are difficult to spell. One word that many people misspell is *receive*. *Receive* is a problem because some people write the *i* before the *e*: *recieve*. The correct spelling is *receive* with the *e* before the *i*. _____

_____

Some people **confuse** *its* with *it's*. In addition, some people write the word *its* with an apostrophe: *its'*. However, this last example is not an English word. Another example of bad spelling is **cemetery**. Some people change the last *e* to *a* because of the pronunciation: *cemetary*. These are just a few of the words that cause spelling problems for native and nonnative English speakers.

confuse: to mix without order   **a cemetery:** a place where people are buried after they die

Missing sentence ideas: <u>Another word is the word *its*.</u> + <u>This word causes spelling problems.</u>

How the Weather Affects Me

Some people do not believe that the weather can **affect** the way you feel, but the weather certainly affects me. On rainy days, I feel like watching a movie or staying in bed. Rainy weather makes me **lazy**. It makes me want to stay inside and take it easy. When the weather is bright and sunny, I feel energetic. This kind of weather makes me want to go outside. I want to play tennis or go to the beach. When the temperature is cool and the sun is shining, I feel like working. I feel **productive**. _____

_____

As you can see, different kinds of weather have different effects on me.

affect: to change in some way   **productive:** able to get things done
lazy: not active

Missing sentence ideas: <u>This is the weather.</u> + <u>I like this weather the most.</u>

Grammar and Sentence Structure

Using Modals to Add Meaning

Writers use **modals** to add extra information to the main verb in the sentence. The modal comes before the main verb, and the main verb is always in its base form. Add *not* after the modal to make it negative. Each modal has a different meaning. Below are some common modals, their meanings, and some example sentences.

Modal	Meaning	Example Sentence
will	to show the future	Next week, Rachel **will travel** to the Ivory Coast.
should	to give advice	It is going to rain. You **should take** an umbrella.
must	to show necessity	You **must have** a visa to visit that country.
might	to show possibility	The weather is good. We **might go** to the beach.
can	to show ability	Roberto **can speak** three languages.

Remember that you cannot use two modals together. For example:

Incorrect: We might **can** go to a new restaurant for dinner.

Correct: We might go to a new restaurant for dinner.

Do not use the word *to* between the modal and the verb.

Incorrect: We might **to** play football tomorrow.

Correct: We might play football tomorrow.

Incorrect: Can you **to** help us with this electricity bill?

Correct: Can you help us with this electricity bill?

Yes/No *Questions*

Modal	+	Subject	+	Main Verb (base form)	+	Other Parts
Will		you		stop		at the store for me?
Should		I		call		my parents tonight?
Must		we		go		to the party? (formal and implies a complaint)
Can		they		drive		us to work?

NOTE: *Might* is rarely used in question form in American English.

Wh- Questions about the Subject of the Sentence

Subject (*Wh*-Word)	+	Modal	+	Main Verb (base form)	+	Other Parts
Who		will		return		the books?
Who		should		pay		for the damage?
What		must		come		at the end of a question?
Who		can		help		us?

Wh- Questions about the Rest of the Sentence

Wh-Word	+	Modal	+	Subject	+	Main Verb (base form)	+	Other Parts
When		will		they		finish		the project?
Where		should		we		go		for dinner?
When		can		you		meet		me?

ACTIVITY 7 Using Modals

Answer the following questions about cooking a dinner for your friends. Use should, must, might, can, *or* will.

1. What should you do before your friends arrive at your house?

   _____

2. What must you do to the food before dinner?

   _____

3. What can your friends do for the dinner?

   _____

4. What might you cook if there are twenty guests?

   _____

5. What will you and your friends do after dinner tonight?

   _____

Read the following paragraph. Underline the modal that best completes each sentence. Sometimes both answers are correct. Be prepared to explain your answers.

EXAMPLE PARAGRAPH 66

Improve Your English More Quickly

Here is some good advice on how to improve your English more quickly. First, you (**1.** must / will) always speak English. This requirement (**2.** will / must) help improve your fluency. Second, you (**3.** should / can) also make friends with a native speaker. Then you (**4.** can / must) talk to your new friend in English all the time. They (**5.** can / will) also correct your mistakes because they know the language well. Third, you (**6.** should / might) read a lot in English. This will improve your vocabulary. Finally, you (**7.** might / should) keep a daily journal. This (**8.** must / will) give you practice writing in English. These suggestions (**9.** should / must) help your English get better more rapidly.

For more practice with modals, try Unit 7, Activity 4 on the *Great Writing 1* Web site: elt.heinle.com/greatwriting

The sentences below have some errors in capitalization and punctuation. First, find and correct the errors in each sentence. After you have corrected the errors, put the sentences in the correct order (1 through 6) to make a good paragraph. The first one has been done for you.

a. ___1___ S̶udan is a country that is in the northeastern part of a̶frica.

b. _____ it is a large country with many different people

c. _____ in conclusion, different areas of this country have very different histories

d. _____ the people who live in the southern part of the country were independent for many years

e. _____ however, the people who live in the northern part of the country were under foreign control for long periods of time

f. _____ some of the countries that ruled this northern area were egypt rome turkey and britain

For more practice with sequencing sentences, try Unit 7, Activity 5 on the *Great Writing 1* Web site: elt.heinle.com/greatwriting

Copy the sentences from Activity 9 in correct paragraph form. Be sure to add a title.

EXAMPLE PARAGRAPH 67

_____

_____

_____

_____

_____

_____

_____

_____

_____

Understanding Place Phrases

You learned that to make a sentence more interesting, it is important to add details such as adjectives and connectors. In Unit 6, you learned that time words can add variety to your sentences. Another way to give more information in a sentence is to add place phrases.

Grammar and Sentence Structure

Prepositional Phrases of Place

Prepositional phrases of place function as adverbs—they modify a verb. They tell *where*. Here are some examples.

at the picnic	on the little table	under the chair	next to the front door
at school	over my head	at home	near the stove

Notice that the phrases begin with small words such as *at, in,* and *on*. These words are called **prepositions**. (See the Brief Writer's Handbook, pages 225–226, for more information about prepositions.) Every preposition in a place phrase needs a noun or a pronoun. This noun or pronoun is called the **object of the preposition**. The combination of the preposition and the object is called a **prepositional phrase**.

Parts of a Prepositional Phrase (Place)				
prepositional phrase	preposition	article (*a, an, the*) OR demonstrative pronoun (*this, that, these, those*) OR possessive pronoun (*my, your, her*, etc.) OR quantifier (*some, any, one, two*, etc.) OR Ø	adjective	noun OR pronoun
at the picnic	at	the		picnic
on that little table	on	that	little	table
next to my friends	next to	my		friends
under two old chairs	under	two	old	chairs
near them	near			them

It is common to put place phrases at the end of a sentence.

Incorrect: We ate <u>at the picnic</u> lots of sandwiches and salad.

Correct: We ate lots of sandwiches and salad <u>at the picnic</u>.

Incorrect: Loretta <u>in my house</u> lives.

Correct: Loretta lives <u>in my house</u>.

Place Phrases and Time Words

In sentences where you have a place phrase and a time word or phrase, remember this rule:

At the end of a sentence, place phrases usually come *before* time words or phrases.

Incorrect: Meet me <u>tomorrow afternoon</u> <u>in the library</u>.
                             TIME WORDS   PLACE PHRASE

Correct: Meet me <u>in the library</u> <u>tomorrow afternoon</u>.
                         PLACE PHRASE   TIME WORDS

Incorrect: She saw him <u>at 8 P.M.</u> <u>at the bank</u>.
                             TIME WORDS PLACE PHRASE

Correct: She saw him <u>at the bank</u> <u>at 8 P.M.</u>
                         PLACE PHRASE TIME WORDS

Correct: <u>At 8 P.M.</u>, she saw him <u>at the bank</u>.
     TIME WORDS   PLACE PHRASE

Read the sentence parts below. Put the parts in the correct order. Then write the complete sentences on the lines provided. **You may have to add articles or verbs to the phrases.** *Use correct capitalization and punctuation. The first one has been done for you.*

1. Lucinda / in ten minutes / going to / drive to / video store

   <u>Lucinda is going to drive to the video store in ten minutes.</u>

2. last week / the Johnson sisters / party / excellent / have

   _____

   _____

3. next Monday / new car / we / buy

   _____

   _____

4. at gym / exercise / Janie / every morning

   _____

   _____

5. did you take / yesterday morning / in Mrs. Smith's class / grammar test

   _____

   _____

6. leave / I / last night / my books / in car

   _____

   _____

7. two days ago / met Luis / they / at restaurant

   _____

   _____

8. Sara / the pie / right now / put / in oven

   _____

   _____

9. at airport / in ten minutes / our friends / arrive

   _____

   _____

10. squirrels / every day / nuts / bury / under our oak tree

_____

_____

ACTIVITY 12 Practicing Adverbs of Place and Time Words

Read the paragraph. It is missing three sentences. Below the paragraph are the parts of the missing sentences. Put the words in each sentence in the correct order. Then write the complete sentences in the spaces provided. You will have to add articles and use the correct verb tense. Remember to use correct capitalization and punctuation.

EXAMPLE PARAGRAPH 68

A Long Flight

(1.) _____

_____

However, Daniel lives in Bogotá, Colombia, so he has to catch a flight to Turkey before the

meeting. Daniel is going to go to the airport today. (2.) _____

_____

Because Daniel is going to take an international flight, he has to be at the airport at 3:00 P.M. If he

does not leave his house by noon, he is going to be late. It is almost 11:30 now. (3.) _____

_____

_____

Then he will leave on his long trip.

1. attend / in Istanbul, Turkey / Daniel / important company meeting / in two days
2. his flight / at 5:00 P.M. / leave / from Gate 32
3. his suitcase / Daniel / put / in ten minutes / in the car

 For more practice with place phrases and time words, try Unit 7, Activity 6 and Activity 7 on the *Great Writing 1* Web site: elt.heinle.com/greatwriting

ACTIVITY 13 Sentence or Fragment Review

Read each group of words. If it is a fragment, write F on the line. If it is a complete sentence or question, write S on the line. The first two have been done for you.

1. __F__ Every year go to the beach in Hawaii.

2. __S__ Johnny has an appointment with a chiropractor at 4:30 P.M.

3. _____ We are going to have a big party to celebrate Mark's next birthday.

4. _____ Ten years to become a medical doctor in the United States.

5. _____ Next Tuesday am going to see the new action movie.

6. _____ Did you get a nice gift for your birthday last week?

7. _____ Wendy is eating lunch and talking to her friends in the cafeteria right now.

8. _____ Because Mira works hard every day.

9. _____ Peru and Argentina Spanish-speaking countries in South America.

10. _____ Ralph left his wallet at his friend's house last night.

ACTIVITY 14 Editing: Grammar and Sentence Review

Read the following paragraph. It contains 10 mistakes: adjective clauses (1), fragments (1), word order of adjectives (1), possessive adjectives (1), commas (2), articles (1), compound sentences (1), and capitalization (2). Find and correct the mistakes. The first one has been done for you.

EXAMPLE PARAGRAPH 69

Visiting a New Country

There are m

~~Many~~ reasons to visit a new country. First, you can see beautiful interesting and distant places. For example, you can visit a Kremlin and Red Square in moscow. Another reason to travel is to eat new types of food. If you visit Thailand, you can drink jasmine tea, you can eat coconut-flavored rice. Finally, you can meet new people which live in these exotic countries. you can talk to people and learn more about his likes and dislikes. As you can see, traveling to another country is important for reasons different.

 For more practice with error correction, try Unit 7, Activity 8 on the *Great Writing 1* Web site: elt.heinle.com/greatwriting

Building Better Sentences

Correct and varied sentence structure is essential to the quality of your writing. For further practice with the sentences and paragraphs in this unit, go to Practice 7 on page 237 in Appendix 1.

Building Better Vocabulary

ACTIVITY 15 Word Associations

Circle the word or phrase that is most closely related to the word or phrase on the left. If necessary, use a dictionary to check the meaning of words you do not know.

1. a suitcase	a thing for holding clothes	a thing for holding money
2. to receive	to give something	to get something
3. evening	night	afternoon
4. a salary	money spent	money earned
5. to improve	to become better	to become worse
6. a flight	a ride in an airplane	a ride on a ship
7. exotic	strange and different	the same and ordinary
8. a journal	a type of writing	a type of speaking
9. distant	very close	far away
10. a district	an area	a government

ACTIVITY 16 Using Collocations

Fill in each blank with the word on the left that most naturally completes the phrase on the right. If necessary, use a dictionary to check the meaning of words you do not know.

1. salary / official	a low _____
2. bright / few	a _____ light
3. hard / hardly	to work _____
4. for / with	to agree _____ someone
5. on / in	to go _____ strike

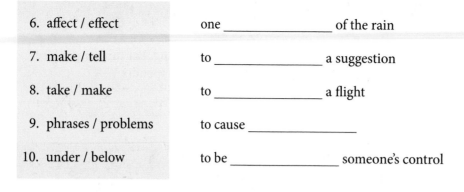

6. affect / effect	one _____ of the rain	
7. make / tell	to _____ a suggestion	
8. take / make	to _____ a flight	
9. phrases / problems	to cause _____	
10. under / below	to be _____ someone's control	

ACTIVITY 17 Parts of Speech

Study the following word forms. In the sentences on the right, choose the best word and write it in the blank space. Be sure to use the correct form of the verb. If necessary, use a dictionary to check the meaning of words you do not know. (NOTE: The word in bold is the original word that appears in the unit.)

Noun	Verb	Adjective	Sentence Practice
assignment	assign	Ø	1. Yesterday's _____ was very easy.
			2. My professor _____ too much homework last night.
energy	energize	**energetic**	3. Carla's son is very _____.
			4. He has a lot of _____.
pronunciation	pronounce	Ø	5. Can you _____ the word *psychology*?
			6. Lee's _____ needs work.
confusion	**confuse**	confused/ confusing	7. There was a lot of _____ at the concert.
			8. The directions for the test were _____.
decision	decide	decisive	9. The president _____ to run for re-election last week.
			10. Bindu made a _____ to drop out of college.

Noun endings: -ment, -tion, -sion

Verb endings: -ize

Adjective endings: -etic, -ed, -ing, -ive

Original Student Writing

In your opinion, which is better—cooking and eating food at home or eating out in a restaurant? Write a paragraph in which you answer this question and tell why.

Follow these steps for writing. Put a check (✓) next to each step as you complete it. When you finish your paragraph, use the checklist that follows to edit your work. You may want to review What Is a Paragraph? *in Unit 2 on page 39.*

Step 1 _____ In your first sentence, tell which type of food you prefer.

Step 2 _____ In the supporting sentences, give two or three reasons why you prefer this type of food.

Step 3 _____ Give details for each reason you give.

Step 4 _____ In the last sentence, summarize your opinion about the type of food that you prefer.

Step 5 _____ Write at least two adjective clauses.

Step 6 _____ Use at least three of the vocabulary words or phrases presented in Activity 15, Activity 16, and Activity 17. Underline these words and phrases in your paragraph.

Step 7 _____ Try to include time words and place phrases in some of the sentences in Step 2 or Step 3.

Step 8 _____ Write at least one compound and one complex sentence in Step 2 or Step 3.

✔ Checklist

1. ❏ Did you use the simple present tense in your paragraph?

2. ❏ Make sure that you use articles correctly.

3. ❏ Check for correct punctuation.

4. ❏ Make sure every sentence has a subject and a verb—no fragments!

5. ❏ Create a title for your paragraph.

Exchange papers from Activity 18 with a partner. Read your partner's writing. Then use Peer Editing Sheet 7 on page 261 to help you comment on your partner's writing. Be sure to offer positive suggestions and comments that will help your partner improve his or her writing. Consider your partner's comments as you revise your own writing.

Additional Topics for Writing

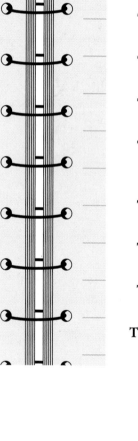

Here are ten ideas for journal writing. Choose one or more of them to write about. Follow your teacher's directions. (We recommend that you skip a line after each line that you write. This gives your teacher a place to write comments.)

TOPIC 1: Write about an animal that you like. Describe the animal, tell where the animal lives, and tell why you like this animal so much.

TOPIC 2: Write about your dream house or apartment. Describe what this house looks like (how many rooms, what type of architecture, etc). Write about the location of the house (in the mountains? on the beach? in a big city?).

TOPIC 3: Organized sports in school help children grow up to become better adults. Do you agree or disagree with this statement? Why?

TOPIC 4: Do you think that young children who know something about computers have an advantage in school today? Why or why not?

TOPIC 5: What is the worst decision that you have ever made? Give details about why it was a bad decision.

TOPIC 6: What is the best decision that you have ever made? Why was it a good decision? Did you come to this decision by yourself? How did you feel after you made this decision?

TOPIC 7: Write about a book that you like. Describe the book, briefly tell what happens in the story, and explain why you like this book.

TOPIC 8: Describe a painting that you like. Who painted it? What is in the painting? Describe the colors. What do you feel when you look at the painting?

TOPIC 9: Describe your favorite kind of shopping. Where do you shop? What do you shop for? What do you like about the experience?

TOPIC 10: Describe your favorite place to visit. Where is this place? When do you go there? Why do you go there?

Timed Writing

How quickly can you write in English? There are many times when you must write quickly—on a test for example. It is important to feel comfortable during those times. Timed-writing practice can make you feel better about writing quickly in English.

Take out a piece of paper. Then read the writing prompt below this paragraph. Your teacher will give you 5 minutes to brainstorm ideas about the topic. You must write 8 to 10 sentences about this topic. You will have 20 minutes to write these sentences. At the end of the 20 minutes, your teacher will collect your work and return it to you later.

> Describe something that is important to you. It can be a person, place, thing, or idea. What is this thing? Why is it important to you? Give examples. Provide as many details as possible.

More Writing

For extra writing practice, see the activities in Unit 8 and Appendix 2.

Review:
More Practice with Sentences and Paragraphs

GOAL: To practice sentence and paragraph skills from Units 1–7

Practice with Sentences and Paragraphs

This unit contains 27 activities for you to practice writing great sentences in great paragraphs. Some activities focus on sentences while others focus on paragraphs.

When you write the paragraphs in this unit, keep these things in mind:

Important Parts of a Paragraph

TOPIC SENTENCE	1. A good paragraph has a topic sentence that states the main idea.
Only ONE TOPIC	2. All of the sentences in the paragraph are about one topic.
INDENTED line	3. The first line of a paragraph is indented.
BODY and SUPPORTING SENTENCES	4. A good paragraph has a sufficient number of supporting sentences.
CONCLUDING SENTENCE	5. The last sentence, or concluding sentence, brings the paragraph to a logical conclusion.

ACTIVITY 1 Basic Punctuation and Capitalization

Read each set of sentences. Correct the punctuation and capitalization errors. Then number the sentences in the correct order. Rewrite the sentences in paragraph form on the lines below. Finally, add a title.

1. a. _____ in fact, the andes affect almost every aspect of peruvian life

 b. _____ it is located in the south-central part of the continent

 c. _____ peru is a country in south America

 d. _____ the andes mountains run through the middle of the country

 e. _____ the mountains affect weather agriculture and transportation

_____

_____

_____

_____

_____

_____

_____

_____

_____

2. a. _____ they are classified as birds but they cannot fly

b. _____ instead, they are excellent swimmers because they have wings shaped like flippers

c. _____ they live only in the cold regions in the southern hemisphere

d. _____ penguins are very interesting animals

e. _____ many people think that these birds live at the north pole but they do not

_____

_____

_____

_____

_____

_____

_____

_____

This activity will help you practice correct noun and adjective forms, verb tenses, and article usage. Read the paragraph. Underline the word that correctly completes each sentence.

EXAMPLE PARAGRAPH 72

The Tomato: Fruit or Vegetable?

In supermarkets, people can find tomatoes in the vegetable section, but this common food is actually a (**1.** fruit / fruits). Many people (**2.** believe / believes) it is a (**3.** vegetable because / vegetable. Because) we eat it with (**4.** others / other) salty foods. For example, we eat (**5.** tomato / tomatoes) in salads and on sandwiches. We do not eat (**6.** tomato / tomatoes) for dessert or with anything sweet. However, the tomato is really a fruit. Now isn't that strange?

For more practice with word forms, try Unit 8, Activity 1 on the *Great Writing 1* Web site: elt.heinle.com/ greatwriting

ACTIVITY 3 Editing in Four Steps

Read this paragraph. Then rewrite it according to the four editing steps on page 191.

EXAMPLE PARAGRAPH 73

Our Family's Koi Pond

Today my father is going to build a koi pond in our backyard. First, he is going to dig a big hole in the center of the yard. Then he is going to lay a sheet of black plastic in the hole. Next, he is going to put rocks around the edge of the hole. After that, he is going to fill the new pond with water. Finally, he is going to add plants and fish. It is going to be a lot of hard work, but he is going to enjoy it.

Make the following changes to the paragraph on page 190. Write your new paragraph on the lines below.

Step 1. In the first sentence, change *my father* to *my father and I*.

Step 2. Change all the pronouns to fit the new subject.

Step 3. In the first sentence, change the word *Today* to *Last Saturday*.

Step 4. Change all the simple future tense verbs to simple past tense verbs.

Our Family's Koi Pond

_____

_____

_____

_____

_____

_____

_____

_____

_____

_____

Read this paragraph. Then rewrite it according to the five editing steps below.

Our First Garden

Two years ago, my brother and I planted our first garden. First, we chose the location of the garden. We put it in a place that gets a lot of sunlight. Then we dug up the ground. After that, we added fertilizer. Next, we took seeds and planted them in rows in the garden. Finally, we watered the new garden. It was hard work, but we are proud of our garden.

Make the following changes to the paragraph above. Write your new paragraph on the lines below.

Step 1. In the first sentence, change *my brother and I* to *Antonio*.

Step 2. Change all the pronouns and possessive adjectives to fit the new subject.

Step 3. In the first sentence, change the phrase *Two years ago* to *Tomorrow*.

Step 4. Change all the simple past tense verbs to simple future tense verbs (*be going to*).

Step 5. Check the other verbs to make sure that they are correct.

Antonio's First Garden

_____

_____

_____

_____

_____

_____

_____

_____

_____

This activity will help you practice choosing the correct verb tense. Read the paragraph. Underline the correct verbs. Then answer the questions that follow the paragraph.

An Important Invention

I (**1.** believe / believed) that the light bulb is one of the most important inventions in the world. In the past, people (**2.** used / are using) candles to see at night. This light was very weak and difficult to see with. However, the light bulb now (**3.** allowed / allows) us to see things easily in the dark. This invention also (**4.** help / helps) us to do more work in one day. Before the light bulb, most work (**5.** ends / ended) at sundown. Now people can continue to work outdoors or in their offices for much longer at night. In addition, people can do more fun things when it is dark. For example, sports fans (**6.** watch / watched) baseball games at night on lighted fields. Music lovers (**7.** listen / are listening) to a concert in a lighted stadium. Without the light bulb, people would not have as many choices for work or play.

1. What is the topic sentence of the paragraph?

   _____

   _____

2. How many sentences does the paragraph have? _____

3. What reasons does the writer give to support the main idea?

   _____

   _____

4. What two verb tenses does the writer use? Why?

   _____

   _____

ACTIVITY 6 Original Writing Practice with Verb Tenses

In Activity 5, you read one writer's opinion about an important invention in history. What do you think is an important invention in history? Write a short paragraph about it. Include a topic sentence and three examples to support your opinion. Create a title for your paragraph.

_____

_____

_____

_____

_____

_____

_____

_____

ACTIVITY 7 Verb Tense

This activity will help you practice choosing the correct verb tense. Read the paragraph. Underline the correct verbs. Then answer the questions on page 195.

EXAMPLE PARAGRAPH 78

A Busy Day

Tomorrow (**1.** is / is going to be) a busy day for me. Usually, I (**2.** get / am getting) up at seven o'clock in the morning. However, tomorrow I (**3.** get / am going to get) up at five o'clock because I am going to go to the gym. After I finish at the gym, I (**4.** go / am going to go) to work. I usually (**5.** start / am starting) work at nine o'clock. Tomorrow I (**6.** start / am going to start) work at eight o'clock. After work, I frequently (**7.** have / am having) dinner with my friends. However, tomorrow I (**8.** go / will go) directly to my mother's house because it is her birthday. We (**9.** have / are going to have) a big party for her. I know I will have a lot of fun tomorrow.

1. What is the topic sentence of the paragraph?

   _____

   _____

2. How many sentences does the paragraph have? _____

3. What reasons does the writer give to support the main idea?

   _____

   _____

4. What two tenses does the writer use? Why?

   _____

   _____

 For more practice with verb tense, try Unit 8, Activity 2 on the *Great Writing 1* Web site: elt.heinle.com/greatwriting

ACTIVITY 8 Original Writing Practice with Verb Tenses

In Activity 7, you read about one person's busy day. Write a paragraph describing a busy day in your life. It can be about a day in the past, present, or future. Include a topic sentence and three examples to support your opinion. Create a title for your paragraph.

_____

_____

_____

_____

_____

_____

_____

_____

_____

_____

Writer's Note

Adding Interest to Your Writing

Remember to use a variety of sentence types (simple, compound, complex) in your writing. Different kinds of sentences will make your writing more interesting. You can also use adverbs and adjectives to add variety and interest to your writing.

ACTIVITY 9 Connecting Sentences in a Paragraph

This activity will help you practice combining sentences with a connector. Combine each underlined pair of sentences. You may use and, but, or so to connect them. Remember to add a comma before the connecting word. You may have to delete some words. Rewrite the paragraph on the lines on page 197.

EXAMPLE PARAGRAPH 79

My First Car

My first car was the best car in the world. It was a Mustang. (**1.**) <u>My Mustang was bright blue</u>. <u>It was very powerful</u>. All my friends were jealous when they saw it. (**2.**) <u>They wanted to drive it</u>. <u>I told them they could not</u>. I said that they could be passengers or pedestrians. (**3.**) <u>My friends did not want to walk</u>. <u>They always chose to be passengers</u>. However, the best thing about my car was the way it made me feel. (**4.**) <u>Every weekend, I drove to the movie theater in that car</u>. <u>Every weekend, my friends rode with me</u>. We felt like movie stars because everyone stared at us in my beautiful blue car. I will never forget the fun that I had in that cool car.

_____

_____

_____

_____

_____

_____

_____

_____

_____

_____

_____

ACTIVITY 10 Editing for Connectors (*and, but, so*)

Follow these instructions:

1. *Reread your writing in Activity 6 and Activity 8. Did you use any connectors in your sentences?*

2. *If so, rewrite those sentences below.*

3. *If not, combine two of your sentences with a connector.*

4. *Ask a partner to check your sentences. Did you use the connectors correctly?*

_____

_____

_____

_____

_____

ACTIVITY 11 Articles

This activity will help you review the correct use of articles. Read the paragraph. Underline the article that correctly completes each sentence. (NOTE: Ø means "no article.")

Shark!

I will never forget my first encounter with (**1.** a / an / Ø) shark. I was nineteen, and I was visiting Australia with my family. My father and I went scuba diving on (**2.** a / the / Ø) Great Barrier Reef. We went out to (**3.** a / the / Ø) reef with many other tourists on (**4.** a / an / the) special boat. When we got to (**5.** a / the / Ø) reef, the scuba diving instructor helped us put on our equipment. Then we dove into (**6.** a / the / Ø) clear blue water. Everything was so beautiful! There were colorful fish and lots of different kinds of coral. I swam everywhere. Suddenly, I saw (**7.** a / an / the) huge gray shark swim towards me. I looked around for my father, but I was far away from him and (**8.** a / an / the) group of tourists. What could I do? (**9.** A / An / The) shark got closer and closer. I was so scared that I could not move. Just when I thought that it might bite me, (**10.** a / an / the) shark turned and swam (**11.** a / the / Ø) other way. Unbelievable! I quickly found my father. Now I never swim off by myself when I go scuba diving.

ACTIVITY 12 Editing for Articles

Follow these instructions:

1. *Reread your writing in Activity 6 and Activity 8.*
2. *Choose three sentences from your paragraphs that contain articles. Write them below.*
3. *Ask a partner to check your sentences. Did you use the articles correctly?*

_____

_____

_____

_____

_____

_____

 For more practice with articles, try Unit 8, Activity 3 on the *Great Writing 1* Web site: elt.heinle.com/greatwriting

ACTIVITY 13 Adjective Clauses with *Who* and *That*

Read the paragraph. Underline the word that correctly completes each sentence. Circle the two unrelated sentences.

EXAMPLE PARAGRAPH 82

How the Months of the Year Got Their Names

The names of all twelve months come from Roman culture and myths. First, there are several months (**1.** that / who) are named after Roman gods and goddesses. The Roman god of beginnings (**2.** that / who) gave us the month of January is Janus. The month (**3.** that / who) got its name from the Roman god of war is March. May and June honor the Roman goddesses Maia and Juno. Some months get their names from festivals. Both February and April come from special celebrations (**4.** that / who) appeared on the old Roman calendar. February usually only has 28 days. Two months (**5.** that / who) come in the summer got their names from Roman emperors. July is the month (**6.** that / who) honors Julius Caesar and August is named for Emperor Augustus. These months are usually hot. Finally, September, October, November, and December are named after the seventh, eighth, ninth, and tenth months of the Roman calendar. The month names (**7.** that / who) are so commonly used today certainly have a very rich history.

 For more practice with adjective clauses with *who* and *that*, try Unit 8, Activity 4 on the *Great Writing 1* Web site: elt.heinle.com/greatwriting

ACTIVITY 14 Editing for Adjective Clauses

Follow these instructions:

1. *Reread your writing in Activity 6 and Activity 8. Did you use adjective clauses in your writing?*
2. *If so, rewrite those sentences below.*
3. *If not, combine two of your sentences using an adjective clause.*
4. *Ask a partner to check your sentences. Did you use the adjective clauses correctly?*

_____

_____

_____

_____

Practice with Sentences and Paragraphs **199**

This activity will help you recognize the difference between a topic sentence and supporting sentences. Each pair of sentences is about one topic. Decide which sentence is the topic sentence (T) and which is a supporting sentence (S). (Hint: The topic sentence gives more general information.)

1. Topic: Kennedy Space Center

    _____ You can visit the Shuttle Plaza and walk through a life-size model of a space shuttle.

    _____ Kennedy Space Center is a great place to visit.

2. Topic: The Definition of Patience

    _____ A teacher often shows patience to young students at the end of the school day.

    _____ Patience is the ability to continue doing something even if you do not see any results immediately.

3. Topic: The Capilano Bridge

    _____ The Capilano Bridge is famous worldwide.

    _____ The Capilano Bridge is 450 feet (137 m) long and rises 230 feet (70 m) above the Capilano River.

4. Topic: Making New Friends

    _____ Some kids tried to be nice to me, but I did not want to talk to them.

    _____ I learned the hard way how to make friends in a new school.

5. Topic: Cell Phones and Driving

    _____ When drivers talk on cell phones, they get distracted and do not pay enough attention to driving.

    _____ One of the recent developments of modern technology—cell phones—can be a threat to safe driving.

For more practice with topic sentences and supporting sentences, try Unit 8, Activity 5 on the *Great Writing 1* Web site: elt.heinle.com/greatwriting

Read all the sentences below. Then put them in a logical paragraph order. When you finish, write the sentences in correct paragraph format on the lines below. Be sure to add an appropriate title.

a. _____ Instead, breakfast for them often consists of eggs with toast and coffee.

b. _____ People in Malaysia eat rice for breakfast, too, but their rice is cooked in coconut milk.

c. _____ Breakfast foods vary from country to country.

d. _____ However, people in most countries in Central and South America do not eat rice for breakfast.

e. _____ People eat this sweet, flavored rice with a red paste that is made of ground chili peppers and other ingredients.

f. _____ In Japan, for example, it is common to eat rice, soup, and fish for breakfast.

g. _____ From these varied breakfast items, it is clear that breakfast foods are different around the world.

For more practice with sentence order in paragraphs, try Unit 8, Activity 6 on the *Great Writing 1* Web site: elt.heinle.com/greatwriting

EXAMPLE PARAGRAPH 83

_____

_____

_____

_____

_____

_____

_____

_____

_____

_____

_____

Discuss the answers to these questions in a small group. Then read the paragraph.

1. Do you like to cook? If so, what is your favorite meal to prepare?

2. How much time do you spend in the kitchen?

3. Have you ever eaten linguine?

EXAMPLE PARAGRAPH 84

Something Easy to Cook

One of the quickest and easiest meals to prepare is linguine with tomato sauce. First, fill a large pot about three-quarters full with water. Bring the water to a boil and add about eight ounces of your favorite linguine. It will take about ten minutes for the pasta to cook thoroughly. While the pasta is cooking, heat a large skillet with about two tablespoons of olive oil. Slice three or four cloves of garlic and add them to the skillet. Stir frequently until the garlic cloves become a golden brown color. Add a large can of tomato sauce to the garlic and oil. Then add a pinch of salt and pepper. When the linguine is done, strain it in a colander and put the linguine in the skillet. Add some grated parmesan cheese and some chopped basil. Your delicious linguine dinner is ready. *Buon appetito!*

Read each question about Example Paragraph 84 in Activity 17. Circle the best answer.

1. What is the main topic of the paragraph?
   a. the health benefits of linguine
   b. why linguine is inexpensive
   c. cooking a quick linguine meal

2. What is the topic sentence of this paragraph?
   a. One of the quickest and easiest meals to prepare is linguine with tomato sauce.
   b. First, fill a large pot about three-quarters full with water.
   c. Add some grated parmesan cheese and some chopped basil.

3. In your opinion, what does the paragraph explain?

    a. It explains why cooking linguine is better than eating fast food.

    b. It tells you that linguine is the easiest and most delicious food to make in the kitchen.

    c. It lists the steps necessary to make a quick linguine dinner.

4. How many (food) ingredients does the author mention in the paragraph?

    a. three

    b. eight

    c. ten

5. Read the paragraph again. What kind of verb is most often used?

    a. simple past

    b. present progressive

    c. commands

Writer's Note

Words That Express an Opinion

When you write about your beliefs on a subject, you are giving your opinion. Here are some words and phrases that you can use when you write about your opinion:

believe	I *believe* that no one should smoke in public.
feel	I *feel* that smoking is a personal decision.
think	I *think* that smoking is bad for your health.
agree	I *agree* with the new laws that prohibit smoking.
disagree	I *disagree* with the new laws that prohibit smoking.
have mixed feelings	I *have mixed feelings* about smoking in public places. (This means the writer has more than one opinion on the topic, and the opinions conflict with each other.)

For practice with sentences that express an opinion, try Unit 8, Activity 7 on the *Great Writing 1* Web site: elt.heinle.com/greatwriting

Responding to Issues in the News

In the following section, you will read paragraphs that discuss topics in the news. You will also read people's opinions on these issues. Then you will write about your opinions.

Read the following paragraph. Then read the opinions that follow and answer the questions.

EXAMPLE PARAGRAPH 85

Smoking in Public Places

In the last two decades, many U.S. cities voted to **ban** smoking in public areas. The main reason for doing this was public health. The action was **controversial** because smokers felt **discriminated against**. Some **activists** believe that **barring** smoking in public **establishments** is not the only solution to the problem. In fact, they propose establishing separate areas for smokers and nonsmokers, installing advanced ventilation systems, and using other measures. However, the **ruling** to ban smoking in public places is now a law.

ban: to prohibit, to make illegal
controversial: causing conflict or debate
discriminated against: judged or acted upon unfavorably
an activist: a person who works to support a political cause

barring: prohibiting, banning
an establishment: a business
a ruling: a decision

Opinion 1

Melinda:

Because secondhand smoke causes cancer, I believe that banning smoking in public places is correct. If smoking is not permitted in government buildings like the post office or courthouse, why should any other public place be different? One day smoking is going to be against the law, so this is not going to be an issue anymore. Until then, smokers should not create an unhealthy environment for people in public places.

1. What is the topic sentence of Melinda's paragraph?

   _____

   _____

2. In your own words, write one sentence about how Melinda feels about this issue.

   _____

   _____

3. What argument does Melinda use to support her opinion?

   _____

Opinion 2

Scott:

I am not a smoker, but I disagree with the new laws that prohibit smoking. I think it is unfair to single out smokers and make them feel unaccepted. People in public places like restaurants are allowed to eat as much greasy, unhealthy food as they want, which can cause a heart attack and other serious health problems. Overeating is just as unhealthy as smoking is, yet only the smokers are punished. Adults should be able to make their own decision about smoking. I think that fewer smokers will want to visit public places as much and businesses will suffer because of this law.

1. What is the topic sentence of Scott's paragraph?

   _____

   _____

2. In your own words, write one sentence about how Scott feels about this issue.

   _____

   _____

3. What argument does Scott use to support his opinion?

   _____

   _____

Opinion 3

Amanda:

I really have mixed feelings about this new law. On the one hand, I am glad that when I go into a restaurant, cigarette smoke does not ruin the smell and flavor of my food. In the past, some restaurants were so smoky that I had to leave because I could not enjoy my food. Now, that will not happen to me again. On the other hand, I believe that there can be a compromise. I go to places like zoos and airports that have special areas for smoking, and I have no problems there. Maybe the two groups can reach a compromise that will satisfy everyone.

1. What is the topic sentence of Amanda's paragraph?

   _____

   _____

2. In your own words, write one sentence about how Amanda feels about this issue.

   _____

   _____

3. How is Amanda's opinion different from Melinda's and Scott's?

   _____

   _____

Should and the Tone of Verbs

You can use the word *should* to soften your verbs when you give your opinion. Study these examples.

Strong: People <u>must</u> not talk on their cell phones in their cars.

Strong: People <u>have to</u> stop talking on their cell phones in their cars.

Softer: People <u>should</u> not talk on their cell phones in their cars.

ACTIVITY 20 Original Writing

Now it is your turn to state your opinion about this issue. Write a paragraph that tells if you support or oppose the idea of banning smoking in restaurants. Indent your paragraph.

Be careful! Make sure that your first sentence (the topic sentence) states your opinion. Include good supporting sentences. Give your paragraph a title.

_____

_____

_____

_____

_____

_____

_____

_____

_____

_____

_____

_____

_____

_____

Editing

Remember that it is very important to edit your writing. When you edit your writing, you find and correct your mistakes. You should also ask other people to edit your work. They may find mistakes that you missed.

(NOTE: See the Brief Writer's Handbook, pages 229–230, for more information on editing your writing.)

ACTIVITY 21 Peer Editing

Exchange books with a partner and look at Activity 20. Read your partner's writing. Then use Peer Editing Sheet 8 on page 263 to help you comment on your partner's writing. Be sure to offer positive suggestions and comments that will help your partner improve his or her writing. Consider your partner's comments as you revise your own writing.

ACTIVITY 22 Responding to a Reading Passage

Read the following paragraph. Then read the opinions that follow and answer the questions.

EXAMPLE PARAGRAPH 86

A Medical Dilemma

Recently, there was a **controversy** in Great Britain involving **conjoined twins**. A woman from Malta gave birth to baby girls. Unfortunately, these girls were attached to each other. The parents, who were very religious, did not want doctors to separate the babies. They said it was murder. The doctors explained that with the operation, one baby would live. Without the operation, both babies would die. The British court made the final decision. The doctors performed the operation, and one of the babies died.

a controversy: a debate or a conflict   **conjoined twins:** twins that are physically attached

Opinion 1

Joseph:

A court must not have more power over someone's children than the family. It is unbelievable that the court forced its decision on this unlucky family. The birth of these girls was a natural event, and it was destiny that they were born conjoined twins. The parents did not want the operation because of their religion. That is a strong enough reason to let the parents make the final decision.

1. What is the topic sentence of Joseph's paragraph?

_____

_____

2. In your own words, write one sentence about how Joseph feels about this case.

_____

_____

3. What argument does Joseph use to support his idea?

_____

_____

Opinion 2

Rebecca:

When a human life is involved, the court must have some power in making the decision. Of course the case of these conjoined twin girls is a tragedy, but modern science could help them! The parents used their religion to make the decision. The court only wanted to save a human life. Maybe the parents did not realize that both little girls would die without the operation. To save one baby, I agree with the court.

1. What is the topic sentence of Rebecca's paragraph?

_____

_____

2. In your own words, write one sentence about how Rebecca feels about this case.

_____

_____

3. What argument does Rebecca use to support her idea?

_____

_____

✎ Writer's Note

Varying Your Vocabulary

Vocabulary is a key part of good writing. Your level of vocabulary is an indication of your English proficiency. The reader's opinion of your writing will be higher if you use better vocabulary. Variety is important. In your paragraphs, try to use synonyms, phrases, and sometimes whole sentences to say the same information in a different way. Avoid using the same words all the time.

ACTIVITY 23 Word Associations

Circle the word or phrase that is most closely related to the word or phrase on the left. If necessary, use a dictionary to check the meaning of words you do not know.

1. transportation	driving	walking
2. an invention	a telephone	a mountain
3. a pedestrian	a walker	a rider
4. a ruling	a feeling	a decision
5. thoroughly	hardly	completely
6. banned	can do something	cannot do something
7. controversial	people disagree	people agree
8. established	started	finished
9. recently	in the near past	in the near future
10. to encounter	to understand or comprehend	to meet or find

ACTIVITY 24 Using Collocations

Fill in each blank with the word on the left that most naturally completes the phrase on the right. If necessary, use a dictionary to check the meaning of words you do not know.

1. section / district	a _____ in the clothing store
2. put / give	to _____ the food in the refrigerator
3. allow / classify	to not _____ smoking in public
4. decision / solution	to make a _____ about something
5. about / against	to discriminate _____ a person
6. for / about	to vote _____ a candidate
7. give / classify	to _____ a ruling in court
8. reach / make	to _____ a compromise
9. from / against	to be banned _____ doing something
10. pedestrians / passengers	_____ on a train

Study the following word forms. In the sentences on the right, choose the best word and write it in the blank space. Be sure to use the correct form of the verb. If necessary, use a dictionary to check the meaning of words you do not know. (NOTE: The word in bold is the original word that appears in the unit.)

Noun	Verb	Adjective	Sentence Practice
transportation	transport	Ø	1. New York City's public _____ is excellent.
			2. A truck driver _____ goods from one place to another.
swimmers/swimming	**swim**	Ø	3. Do you like the sport of _____?
			4. _____ have very muscular bodies.
differ**ence**	differ	**different**	5. The twins _____ in their political views.
			6. There is a small _____ between British English and American English.
power	Ø	**powerful**	7. My car's engine does not have the _____ to drive up the mountain.
			8. Joann gave a very _____ speech.
disagree**ment**	**disagree**	disagree**able**	9. There was a _____ between the coach and his players.
			10. Many people _____ about the correct way to load a dishwasher.

Noun endings: -ation, -er, -ing, -ence, -ment

Adjective endings: -ent, -ful, -able

Original Student Writing

ACTIVITY 26 Original Writing

Reread Example Paragraph 86 in Activity 22. Then reread the two opinions and review your answers. Write a paragraph that states <u>your</u> opinion about this case. Tell if you agree or not with what the court decided about the twins Use at least three of the vocabulary words or phrases presented in Activity 23, Activity 24, and Activity 25. Underline these words and phrases in your paragraph.

Be careful! Make sure that the first sentence you write (topic sentence) states the opinion you agree with. Include good supporting sentences. Give your paragraph a title.

_____

ACTIVITY 27 Peer Editing

Exchange books with a partner and look at Activity 26. Read your partner's writing. Then use Peer Editing Sheet 9 on page 265 to help you comment on your partner's writing. Be sure to offer positive suggestions and comments that will help your partner improve his or her writing. Consider your partner's comments as you revise your own writing.

More Writing ———————————————

For extra writing practice, see the activities in Appendix 2.

Brief Writer's Handbook

Definitions of Useful Language Terms

Adjective
An adjective is a word that describes a noun.

Lexi is a very smart girl.

Adverb
An adverb is a word that describes a verb or an adjective.

The secretary types quickly.

Article
The definite article is *the*. The indefinite articles are *a* and *an*.

The teacher gave an assignment to the students.

Jillian is eating a banana.

Clause
A clause is a group of words that has a subject-verb combination. Sentences can have one or more clauses.

Roger wants to go to Harvard University. (one clause)
SUBJ. VERB

Christopher needs to write his report because he wants to pass the class.
SUBJ. VERB   SUBJ. VERB
CLAUSE 1   CLAUSE 2

Noun
A noun is a person, place, thing, or idea.

Sandra likes to eat sandwiches for lunch.

Love is a very strong emotion.

Object
An object is a word that comes after a transitive verb or a preposition.

Jim bought a new car.

I left my jacket in the house.

Predicate
A predicate is the part of a sentence that shows what a subject does.

Mr. Johnston walked to the park.
SUBJECT   PREDICATE

My neighbor's cat was digging a hole in the yard.
SUBJECT   PREDICATE

Preposition
A preposition is a word that can show location, time, and direction. Some common prepositions are *around, at, behind, between, from, on, in, near, to, over, under,* and *with.* Prepositions can also consist of two words (*next to*) or three words (*in addition to*).

Punctuation
Punctuation includes the period (.), comma (,), question mark (?), and exclamation point (!).

Subject
The subject of a sentence tells who or what the sentence is about.

My science teacher gave us a homework assignment. It was difficult.

Tense	A verb has tense. Tense shows when the action happened.
	Simple Present: She <u>walks</u> to school every day.
	Present Progressive: She <u>is walking</u> to school now.
	Simple Past: She <u>walked</u> to school yesterday.
	Past Progressive: She <u>was walking</u> to school when she saw her friend.
	Future: She <u>is going to walk</u> to school tomorrow.
	Future: She <u>will walk</u> to school tomorrow.
Verb	A verb is a word that shows the action of a sentence.
	They <u>speak</u> French.
	My father <u>works</u> at the power plant.

Review of Verb Tenses

Verb Tense	Affirmative	Negative	Usage
Simple Present	I work you take he studies she does we play they have	I do not work you do not take he does not study she does not do we do not play they do not have	• for routines, habits, and other actions that happen regularly • for facts and general truths
Simple Past	I worked you took he studied she did we played they had	I did not work you did not take he did not study she did not do we did not play they did not have	• for actions that are finished • for facts
Present Progressive	I am working you are taking he is studying she is doing we are playing they are having*	I am not working you are not taking he is not studying she is not doing we are not playing they are not having*	• for actions that are happening now • for future actions if a future time adverb is used or understood
Simple Future (*be going to*)	I am going to work you are going to take he is going to study she is going to do we are going to play they are going to have	I am not going to work you are not going to take he is not going to study she is not going to do we are not going to play they are not going to have	• for future actions

Verb Tense	Affirmative	Negative	Usage
Simple Future (*will*)	I will work you will take he will study she will do we will play they will have	I will not work you will not take he will not study she will not do we will not play they will not have	• for future actions
Present Perfect	I have worked you have taken he has studied she has done we have played they have had	I have not worked you have not taken he has not studied she has not done we have not played they have not had	• for actions that began in the past and continue until the present • for actions in the indefinite past time • for repeated actions in the past
Past Progressive	I was working you were taking he was studying she was doing we were playing they were having*	I was not working you were not taking he was not studying she was not doing we were not playing they were not having*	• for longer actions that are interrupted by other actions or events

*Have can be used in progressive tenses only when it has an active meaning in special expressions, such as
- *have* a party
- *have* a good time
- *have* a bad time
- *have* a baby

Capitalization Rules

1. The first word in a statement or question is capitalized.

   I go to the movies every week.

   Do you like to play tennis?

2. The pronoun *I* is always capitalized.

   Larry and **I** are brothers.

3. People's formal and professional titles begin with capital letters.

   Mr. and **Mrs.** Jenkins are on vacation.

   Lisa saw **Dr.** Johansen at the bank yesterday.

4. Proper names (specific people and places) begin with capital letters.

   The **Coliseum** in **Rome** is a beautiful old monument.

   Irene met her brother **Don** at the park.

5. Names of streets begin with capital letters.

   Ruth lives on **Wilson Avenue**.

6. Geographical locations (cities, states, countries, continents, lakes, and rivers) begin with capital letters.

   I am going to travel to **London**, **England**, next week.
   The **Arno River** passes through **Tuscany**, **Italy**.

7. The names of languages and nationalities begin with capital letters.

   My grandmother speaks **Polish**.
   Jessica is going to learn **Japanese**.
   Melissa is **Venezuelan**, but her husband is **Cuban**.

8. Most words in titles of paragraphs, essays, and books are capitalized. The first letter of a title is always capitalized, and the other important words in a title are capitalized. Do not capitalize prepositions (*to, in*), conjunctions (*and, but*), or articles (*a, an, the*) unless they are the first word of the title.

   The Life of Billy Barnes
   Crime and Punishment
   The Catcher in the Rye
   In the Bedroom

9. Specific course names are capitalized.

   Are you taking **History 101** at 10:00 A.M.?
   Are you taking history this semester? (general subject—no capital letter)

Spelling Rules for Regular Simple Past Tense Verbs

1. Add *-ed* to the base form of most verbs.

start	started
finish	finished
wash	washed

2. Add only *-d* when the base form ends in an *e*.

live	lived
care	cared
die	died

3. If a verb ends in a consonant + *y*, change the *y* to *i* and add *-ed*.

dry	dried
carry	carried
study	studied

4. If a verb ends in a vowel + *y*, do not change the *y*. Just add *-ed*.

play	played
stay	stayed
destroy	destroyed

5. If a verb has one syllable and ends in a consonant + vowel + consonant (CVC), double the final consonant and add *-ed*.

stop	sto**pp**ed
CVC	
rob	ro**bb**ed
CVC	

6. If a verb ends in a *w* or *x*, do not double the final consonant. Just add *-ed*.

sew	sewed
mix	mixed

7. If a verb that ends in CVC has two syllables and the <u>second</u> syllable is stressed, double the final consonant and add *-ed*.

ad mit′	admi**tt**ed
oc cur′	occu**rr**ed
per mit′	permi**tt**ed

8. If a verb that ends in CVC has two syllables and the <u>first</u> syllable is stressed, do *not* double the final consonant. Just add *-ed*.

hap′ pen	happened
lis′ ten	listened
o′ pen	opened

Irregular Simple Past Tense Verbs

These are some of the more common irregular verbs in English.

Base Form	Simple Past
be (am/is/are)	was/were
become	became
begin	began
bite	bit
bleed	bled
blow	blew
break	broke
bring	brought
build	built
buy	bought
catch	caught
choose	chose
come	came
cost	cost
cut	cut
do	did
drink	drank
drive	drove
eat	ate
fall	fell
feel	felt
fight	fought
find	found
flee	fled
forget	forgot
get	got
give	gave
grow	grew
have	had
hear	heard
hide	hid
hit	hit
hold	held

Base Form	Simple Past
hurt	hurt
keep	kept
know	knew
leave	left
let	let
lose	lost
make	made
pay	paid
put	put
read	read
run	ran
say	said
see	saw
sell	sold
send	sent
set	set
sing	sang
sit	sat
sleep	slept
speak	spoke
spend	spent
stand	stood
steal	stole
swim	swam
take	took
teach	taught
tell	told
think	thought
throw	threw
understand	understood
wear	wore
win	won
write	wrote

Spelling of the *-ing* (Present Participle) Form of Verbs

1. Add *-ing* to the base form of most verbs.

catch	catching
wear	wearing
go	going

2. If a verb ends in a consonant + *e*, drop the *e* and then add *-ing*.

write	writing
drive	driving
take	taking

3. If a verb has one syllable and ends in a consonant + vowel + consonant (CVC), double the final consonant and add *-ing*.

run CVC	running
sit CVC	sitting
stop CVC	stopping

4. If a verb ends in a *w*, *x*, or *y*, do not double the final consonant. Just add *-ing*.

sew	sewing
mix	mixing
say	saying

5. If a verb that ends in CVC has two syllables and the <u>second</u> syllable is stressed, double the final consonant and add *-ing*.

be gin′	beginning
ad mit′	admitting
re fer′	referring

6. If a verb that ends in CVC has two syllables and the <u>first</u> syllable is stressed, do *not* double the final consonant. Just add *-ing*.

o′ pen	opening
lis′ ten	listening
hap′ pen	happening

Common Stative (Non-action) Verbs

Below is a list of common stative, or non-action, verbs. In general, these verbs do not use the progressive tense because they do not show an action, so they rarely have –*ing*.

Incorrect: She is drinking coffee because she **is disliking** green tea.

Correct: She is drinking coffee because she **dislikes** green tea.

Common Stative (Non-action) Verbs			
agree	hear	own	taste
be	know	prefer	think
believe	like	remember	understand
cost	love	see	want
dislike	mean	seem	
hate	need	smell	

Definite Article *The*

Use the article *the* when you are writing about a specific noun.

1. Use *the* for the second (and subsequent) time you write about something.

    I bought a new ‾coat‾ yesterday. **The** ‾coat‾ is blue and gray.

2. Use *the* when the writer and the reader both know about or are familiar with the subject.

    Are you going to **the bank** this afternoon?

    (Both the writer and the reader know which bank they are talking about.)

3. Use *the* when the noun you are referring to is unique—there is only one.

    The Sun and **the** Earth are both in **the** Milky Way Galaxy.

    The Eiffel Tower is a beautiful monument.

4. Use *the* with specific time periods.

    You must be very quiet for **the** next hour.

5. Use *the* when the other words in your sentence make the noun specific.

    The cat in the picture is very pretty. (*In the picture* specifies which cat you are talking about.)

6. Do not use *the* before names or when you talk about something in general.

Mikhail Bulgakov is a famous Russian writer.

Jason is going to make a table with wood.

7. Some geographic locations require *the*, but others do not. Cities, states, countries, continents, and lakes do not use *the*.

Sylvie is from Venezuela. She lives near Lake Maracaibo.
      COUNTRY NAME   LAKE NAME

However, if the location ends in *-s* (plural), or the words *united, union, kingdom,* or *republic* are in the name of the country, use *the*.

We are going to **the** Bahamas for our vacation. (The country name ends with *-s*.)
Who is the president of **the** United States? (*United* is in the country name.)

Most buildings, bodies of water (except lakes), mountain chains, and deserts use *the*.

The White House is in Washington, D.C.
BUILDING NAME

The Amazon is a very long river in South America.
RIVER NAME

Lake Baikal is a large freshwater lake in Russia.
LAKE NAME
(NO *THE*)

Common Non-count Nouns

Count nouns can be counted: *three* dogs, *two* computers, *one* house, *ten* tomatoes. A non-count noun cannot be counted. Study these commonly used non-count nouns.

Food Items:	butter, sugar, salt, pepper, soup, rice, fish, meat, flour, bread
Liquids:	milk, coffee, water, juice, cream
School Subjects:	English, math, science, music, biology
Abstract Ideas:	love, honesty, poverty, crime, advice, luck, pain, hate, beauty, humor
Others:	homework, information, money, furniture, traffic

NOTE: Non-count nouns use quantifiers such as *much* and *a little*.*

We do not have much time to finish the assignment.

Can you give me a little water? I am thirsty.

Count nouns use quantifiers such as *many* and *a few*.*

There are many cars in the parking lot.

Dayna only has a few dollars in her wallet.

*See Quantifiers on page 224 for more information.

Possessive Adjectives

In general, subject pronouns come before the main verb in a sentence. Possessive adjectives come before a noun.

Subject Pronoun	Possessive Adjective	Example
I	my	I went to Rome last summer with my family.
you (singular)	your	You ate your ice cream already!
he	his	Bill wanted to play soccer. He called his friends.
she	her	Ana rushed to class, so she forgot her cell phone at home.
it	its	The bird fell. It hurt its wing.
we	our	My family and I went on a trip. We visited our relatives.
you (plural)	your	The boss told the workers, "You must do your work quickly."
they	their	The students enjoyed class. They liked their teacher.

Quantifiers

Quantifiers give more information about the quantity, or number, of a noun. Quantifiers usually go in front of a noun. Here are some common examples.

Quantifier	Example
Count	
one, two, three (all numbers) a few few many another several a pair of a couple of	Several students went to the school office. Many people wanted to leave the city. Elizabeth put a few coins in the parking meter.
Non-count	
a little little much	There is only a little milk left in the refrigerator. Hurry! We do not have much time.
Count or Non-count	
some (quantity meaning only) any a lot of the other other	They got into a lot of trouble. Mrs. Jones has a lot of friends. Joanne does not have any money.

The Prepositions *At, On,* and *In*

Prepositions express different ideas. They can indicate time, location, and direction. Remember that a preposition is usually followed by a noun (or pronoun).

Three very common prepositions in English are *at, on,* and *in.* In general, we use *at* with small, specific times and places, *on* with middle-sized times and places, and *in* with larger, more general times and places.

	Time	Place
Small	**at** 1:00 P.M.	**at** the bus stop
Middle	**on** Monday	**on** Bayview Avenue
Big	**in** July **in** spring **in** 2004 **in** this century	**in** Toronto **in** Ontario **in** Canada **in** North America

The Preposition *At*

Location

Use *at* for specific locations.

Angela works **at** the First National Bank.

I always do my homework **at** my desk.

Jeff met Joanne **at** the corner of Polk Street and Florida Avenue.

Time

Use *at* for specific times.

My grammar class meets **at** 9:00 A.M. every day.

I'll see you **at** noon for lunch!

Carla does not like to walk alone **at** night.

Direction

Use *at* for motion toward a goal.

My brother threw a ball **at** me.

The robber pointed his gun **at** the policewoman.

The Preposition *On*

Location

Use *on* when there is contact between two objects. We also use *on* with streets.

The picture is **on** the wall.

He put his books **on** the kitchen table.

Candice lives **on** Bayshore Boulevard.

Time

Use *on* with specific days or dates.

Our soccer game is **on** Saturday.

Your dentist appointment is **on** October 14.

I was born **on** June 22, 1988.

The Preposition *In*

Location

Use *in* when something is inside another thing.

The books are **in** the big box.

I left my jacket **in** your car.

Barbara lives **in** Istanbul.

Time

Use *in* for a specific period of time, a specific year, or a future appointment.

I am going to graduate from college **in** three years.

My best friend got married **in** 2006.

Mr. Johnson always drinks four cups of coffee **in** the morning.

We will meet you **in** ten minutes.

More Prepositions

Here are a few more common prepositions. Remember that a preposition is usually followed by a noun (or pronoun).

with	to	for	by	near	under	from

Examples:

I am going **to** France **with** my cousin.

Marta bought a gift **for** her grandmother.

Please put that box **by** the door.

The student union is **near** my dorm.

Pedro keeps his shoes **under** his bed.

Did you get a job offer **from** that company?

Connectors
Coordinating Conjunctions

Coordinating conjunctions are used to connect two independent clauses (sentences).

NOTE: A comma usually appears before a coordinating conjunction that separates two independent clauses. (An exception is when the two clauses are both very short.)

Purpose	Coordinating Conjunction	Example
To show reason	for*	He ate a sandwich, <u>for</u> he was hungry.
To add information	and	Carla lives in Toronto, <u>and</u> she is a student.
To add negative information	nor**	Roberto does not like opera, <u>nor</u> does he enjoy hip-hop.
To show contrast	but†	The exam was difficult, <u>but</u> everyone passed.
To give a choice	or	We can eat Chinese food, <u>or</u> we can order a pizza.
To show concession/contrast	yet†	The exam was difficult, <u>yet</u> everyone passed.
To show result	so	It was raining, <u>so</u> we decided to stay home last night.

*The conjunction *for* is not common in English. It may be used in literary writing, but it is almost never used in spoken English.

**Notice that question word order is used in the clause that follows *nor*.

†The conjunctions *but* and *yet* have similar meanings. However, *yet* is generally used to show a stronger contrast.

Many writers remember these conjunctions with the acronym *FANBOYS*. Each letter represents one conjunction: F = *for*, A = *and*, N = *nor*, B = *but*, O = *or*, Y = *yet*, and S = *so*.

Subordinating Conjunctions

Subordinating conjunctions are used to connect a dependent clause and an independent clause.

NOTE: When the sentence begins with the dependent clause, a comma should be used after the clause.

Purpose	Subordinating Conjunction	Example
To show reason/cause	because since as	He ate a sandwich <u>because</u> he was hungry. <u>Since</u> he was hungry, he ate a sandwich. <u>As</u> he was hungry, he ate a sandwich.
To show contrast	although even though though while	<u>Although</u> the exam was difficult, everyone passed. <u>Even though</u> the exam was difficult, everyone passed. <u>Though</u> the exam was difficult, everyone passed. Deborah is a dentist <u>while</u> John is a doctor.
To show time relationship	after before until while as	<u>After</u> we ate dinner, we went to a movie. We ate dinner <u>before</u> we went to a movie. I will not call you <u>until</u> I finish studying. <u>While</u> the pasta is cooking, I will cut the vegetables. <u>As</u> I was leaving the office, it started to rain.
To show condition	if even if	<u>If</u> it rains tomorrow, we will stay home. We will go to the park <u>even if</u> it rains tomorrow.

Some Common Comma Rules

1. Put a comma before *and, but, for, or, nor, so,* and *yet* when they connect two independent clauses.

   Richard bought Julie a croissant, but he ate it himself.

2. Put a comma between three or more items in a series.

   Jennifer brought a towel, an umbrella, some sunscreen, and a book to the beach.

3. Put a comma after a dependent clause (a clause that begins with a subordinating conjunction) when that clause begins a sentence.

   Because it was raining outside, Alex used his umbrella.

4. Put a comma before or after the name of a person spoken to.

   "Hamad, do you want to play soccer?" Ana asked.

   "Do you want to play soccer, Hamad?" Ana asked.

5. Commas separate parts of dates and places. Put a comma between the day and the date. Put a comma between the date and the year. Put a comma between a city and a state or a country.

   I was born on Tuesday, June 27, 1989.

   The concert was in Pusan, Korea.

   The headquarters of that company is located in Osaka, Japan.

6. Use a comma to separate an introductory word or phrase from the rest of the sentence.

   Finally, they decided to ask the police for help.

   Every afternoon after school, I go to the library.

   NOTE: *Then* is not followed by a comma.

7. Put a comma to separate information that is not necessary in a sentence.

   Rome, which is the capital of Italy, has a lot of pollution.

   George Washington, the first president of the United States, was a military officer.

8. Put a comma after the salutation in personal letters and after the conclusion in personal and business letters.

   Dear Roberta,   Dear Dr. Gomez,   Dear Ms. Kennedy,

   With love,   Sincerely,   Yours truly,
   Grandma   Jonathan   Alicia

Order of Adjectives

Adjectives can go before nouns.

He has a <u>white</u> car. It is a <u>new</u> car.

When more than one adjective is used before a noun, there is a certain order for the adjectives.

Incorrect: He has a white new car.

Correct: He has a new white car.

In general, there are seven kinds of adjectives. They are used in this order:

1. size — *small, large, huge*
2. opinion — *beautiful, nice, ugly*
3. shape — *round, square, oval*
4. condition — *broken, damaged, burned*
5. age — *old, young, new*
6. color — *red, white, green*
7. origin — *French, American, Korean*

It is common to have two adjectives before a noun but rare to have three or more adjectives before a noun. When there is more than one adjective before a noun, follow the order above. The noun always goes last. Remember that this list is only a general guideline.

Incorrect: a white small Japanese truck

Correct: a small white Japanese truck

Incorrect: a broken large dish

Correct: a large broken dish

Editing Your Writing

While you must be comfortable writing quickly, you also need to be comfortable with improving your work. Writing an assignment is not always a one-step process. It is often a multiple-step process. During your timed writings in Units 3–7, you probably made some changes to your work to make it better. However, you may not have fixed all of the errors. The paper that you turned in to your teacher is called a **first draft**, which is sometimes referred to as a **rough draft**.

A first draft can often be improved. One way to improve your writing is to ask a classmate, friend, or teacher to read it and make suggestions. Your reader may discover that your paragraph is missing a topic sentence or that there are grammar mistakes. You may not always like or agree with your reader's comments, but being open to suggestions will make you a better writer.

This section will help you become more familiar with how to identify and correct errors in your writing.

Step 1

Below is a student's first draft for a timed writing. The writing prompt for this assignment was "Write about a very happy or a very sad event in your life." As you read the first draft, look for areas that need improvement and write your comments in the margin. For example, does every sentence have a subject and a verb? Does the writer always use the correct verb tense and the correct punctuation? Does the paragraph have a topic sentence with controlling ideas?

My Saddest Day

The day I came for the U.S. is my saddest. That night my family gave me a big party. We staied

up all night. In the morning, all the people were go to the airport. We cryed and said good-bye.

they kissed and huged me. i think i will not see them ever again. i was sad in united states for

six months. now i feel better. that was my saddest day.

Step 2

Read the teacher comments on the first draft of "My Saddest Day." Are these the same things that you noticed?

My Saddest Day

Remember
to indent   was
The day I came for the U.S. (is) my saddest. That night my family gave me a big party. We (staied)

There is no "be" form with simple past
up all night. In the morning, all the people (were go) to the airport. We (cryed) and said good-bye.

Always put "the" in front of "United States"
they kissed and (huged) me. i (think) that i will not see them ever again. i was sad in united states

for six months. now i feel better. that was my saddest day.

You have some good ideas in this paragraph. I really like your topic sentence and concluding sentence. However, you write about three different time frames. You write about the night you left your country, the day you arrived in the United States, and six months after you arrived. Choose one of these times and write about that. I'd really like to learn about your party.

Verbs: You must review the spelling rules for the simple past tense. You had a very hard time with this. Also, be careful with irregular forms. The incorrect forms distract from your ideas. I corrected your first mistake. Fix the others I've circled.

I underlined some capitalization errors. Please fix these, too.

Step 3

Now read the second draft of this paper. How is it the same as the first draft? How is it different? Did the writer fix all the sentence mistakes?

My Saddest Party

The night before I came for the U.S. was my saddest party. That night my family gave me a big party. All my family and friends were come to it. We sang, danced, and ate many food. We stayed up all night. We talked about my new life. When everyone left, we cried and said good-bye. They kissed and hugged me. I think I will not see them ever again. Finally, I went to bed at 4:00 in the morning. However, I could not sleep because I was so sad. I was sad in the United States for six months. Now I feel better, but that was my saddest day.

Appendices

Appendix 1

 Building Better Sentences

Being a good writer involves many skills including correct grammar usage, varied vocabulary, and conciseness. Some student writers like to keep their sentences simple. They feel that they will make mistakes writing longer, more complicated sentences. However, writing short choppy sentences one after the other is not considered appropriate in academic writing. Study the examples below.

The time was yesterday.

It was afternoon.

There was a storm.

The storm was strong.

The movement of the storm was quick.

The storm moved towards the coast.

The coast was in North Carolina.

Notice that every sentence has an important piece of information. A good writer would not write all these sentences separately. Instead, the most important information from each sentence can be used to create ONE longer, coherent sentence.

Read the sentences again; this time, the important information has been circled.

The time was yesterday.

It was afternoon.

There was a storm.

The storm was strong.

The movement of the storm was quick.

The storm moved towards the coast.

The coast was in North Carolina.

Here are some strategies for taking the circled information and creating a new sentence.

1. Create time phrases to begin or end a sentence: *yesterday + afternoon*
2. Find the key noun: *storm*
3. Find key adjectives: *strong*
4. Create noun phrases: *a strong + storm*
5. Change word forms: *movement = move; quick = quickly*

   moved + quickly
6. Create place phrases: *towards the coast*

   towards the coast (of North Carolina)

   or

   towards the North Carolina coast

Better Sentence:

Yesterday afternoon, a strong storm moved quickly towards the North Carolina coast.

Here are some other strategies for building better sentences.

7. Use connectors and transition words.

8. Use pronouns as referents for previously mentioned information.

9. Use possessive adjectives and pronouns.

Study the following example.

(Susan)(went) somewhere. That place was(the mall.)Susan wanted to(buy new shoes.)The shoes were for (Susan's mother.)

Improved, Longer Sentence:

Susan went to the mall because she wanted to buy new shoes for her mother.

Practices

This section contains practice for the sentences and paragraphs in Units 1–7. Follow these steps for each practice:

Step 1 Read the sentences. Circle the most important information in each sentence.

Step 2 Write an original sentence from the information you circled. Use the strategies listed on pages 232–233.

Step 3 Go back to the page in the unit to check your sentence. Find the sentence on that page. Compare your sentence with the original sentence. Remember that there is more than one way to combine sentences.

Note that the first exercise in Practice 1 has been done for you.

Practice 1   Unit 1

A. page 7

   1.(John) is my(friend.)

   2. John(works.)

   3. The work is in(Chicago.)

      My friend John works in Chicago.

B. page 3

   1. There are boxes.

   2. The boxes are on the table.

   3. The boxes are heavy.

C. page 24

   1. Caroline attends classes.

   2. The classes are at Jefferson Community College.

   3. The classes are on Wednesdays.

D. page 27

    1. Tuscany is a region.

    2. This region is in Italy.

    3. This region is beautiful.

_____

_____

Practice 2 Unit 2

A. page 37

    1. There are books.

    2. The books are rare.

    3. The books are in the library.

_____

_____

B. page 45

    1. Drivers have more accidents.

    2. The accidents happen on roads.

    3. The roads are snowy.

_____

_____

C. page 60

    1. Aspirin is good for headaches.

    2. Aspirin is good for colds.

    3. Aspirin is good for pain.

_____

_____

Practice 3 Unit 3

A. page 67

    1. Charlie is a man.

    2. Charlie is wonderful.

    3. Charlie is my uncle.

_____

_____

B. page 79

   1. Gretchen studies veterinary medicine.

   2. She studies at the University of Florida.

   3. The University of Florida is in Gainesville.

   _____

   _____

C. page 82 (Hint: Use a coordinating conjunction.)

   1. The students take a test.

   2. The test happens every Friday.

   3. There are scores.

   4. The scores are not very high.

   _____

   _____

Practice 4 Unit 4

A. page 96 (Hint: Use a coordinating conjunction.)

   1. The government in Hunan was corrupt.

   2. Lao-Tzu decided to leave.

   3. Lao-Tzu left his home.

   _____

   _____

B. page 104 (Hint: Use a coordinating conjunction.)

   1. My parents were not rich.

   2. My parents were always happy.

   _____

   _____

C. page 111

   1. This book gives us information.

   2. There is a lot of information.

   3. The book gives us the information now.

   4. The information is important.

   5. The information is about life in the fourteenth century.

   _____

   _____

Practice 5 Unit 5

A. page 119 (Hint: Use a coordinating conjunction.)

1. Mr. Jimenez loves monkeys.

2. Rosario loves monkeys.

3. Mr. Jimenez and Rosario are walking around the exhibit.

4. The exhibit is about monkeys.

_____

_____

B. page 124 (Hint: Use a coordinating conjunction.)

1. Bolivia is a country.

2. Bolivia is landlocked.

3. Bolivia is in South America.

4. Switzerland is a country.

5. Switzerland is landlocked.

6. Switzerland is in Europe.

_____

_____

C. page 130 (Hint: Use a coordinating conjunction.)

1. There are many great places to visit.

2. These places are in this city.

3. You cannot see all these places.

4. This cannot happen in one day.

_____

_____

Practice 6 Unit 6

A. page 146

1. First, Carmen arrives.

2. Then Carmen will perform some dances.

3. These dances will be formal.

4. Carmen is going to do these dances with her friends.

_____

_____

B. page 157

    1. I go to the theater.

    2. The theater is on Broadway.

    3. I do this often.

    4. The reason I do this is that I live in New York.

_____

_____

C. page 160

    1. First, I will arrive in Canada.

    2. Next, I will buy many souvenirs.

    3. There will be souvenirs for my parents.

    4. There will be souvenirs for my brother.

    5. There will be souvenirs for my friends.

_____

_____

Practice 7   Unit 7

A. page 169

    1. The two women are my mother and grandmother.

    2. The women are sitting on the sofa.

_____

_____

B. page 173

    1. These are words.

    2. There are just a few of these words.

    3. These words cause spelling problems for English speakers.

    4. These speakers are native and nonnative.

_____

_____

C. page 182

    1. Wendy is eating lunch.

    2. Wendy is talking to her friends.

    3. Wendy is in the cafeteria.

    4. Wendy is doing these things right now.

_____

_____

Appendix 2

Extra Writing Activities

Writing Activity 1 Writing a Paragraph (Unit 2)

Read the paragraph and follow the steps below to create a new paragraph. Write the new paragraph on the lines provided.

EXAMPLE PARAGRAPH 87

California

[1]California is a large state. [2]It is located in the western part of the United States. [3]The population of California is approximately 36 million. [4]The biggest cities in California are Los Angeles and San Francisco. [5]Millions of tourists visit this state every year. [6]They come for the beaches, the mountains, and the cities that this large state is famous for.

---

1. In Sentences 1, 3, and 4, change *California* to *Florida*. Do the same for the title.
2. In Sentence 2, change *western* to *southeastern*.
3. In Sentence 3, change the population number from *36 million* to *18 million*.
4. In Sentence 4, change the names of the cities from *Los Angeles and San Francisco* to *Miami, Tampa, and Orlando*.
5. In Sentence 6, change *mountains* to *parks*.
6. In Sentence 6, change *cities* to *great weather*.

Writing Activity 2 Writing a Paragraph (Unit 2)

Read the paragraph and follow the steps below to create a new paragraph. Write the new paragraph on the lines provided.

My Older Sister

¹I would like to tell you about my older sister. ²Her name is Natalie. ³She is 26 years old. ⁴She is an elementary school teacher. ⁵She loves children. ⁶She is very patient and kind. ⁷My sister Natalie is a wonderful person.

1. In Sentences 1 and 7, change *sister* to *brother*. Do the same for the title.
2. In Sentences 3, 4, 5, and 6, change *she* to *he*.
3. In Sentence 2, change *her* to *his*. Be sure to use a capital letter.
4. *Natalie* is a girl's name. In Sentences 2 and 7, change *Natalie* to a boy's name of your choice.
5. In sentence 7, change *wonderful* to *great*.

Writing Activity 3 Writing a Paragraph (Unit 2)

Read the paragraph and follow the steps below to create a new paragraph. Write the new paragraph on the lines provided. The current title is simple. Write a better or more interesting title for your paragraph.

My House

[1]I live in a big house. [2]It is located on Princeton Street. [3]My house number is 915. [4]My house is new. [5]It is two years old. [6]The sides of my house are light yellow. [7]The roof is light gray. [8]In front of the house, there are many flowers. [9]I am so lucky to live in this house!

1. In Sentence 1, change *big* to *little*.
2. In Sentence 2, change the name of the street from *Princeton Street* to *Hillside Road*.
3. In Sentence 3, change the house number from *915* to *710*.
4. In Sentence 4, change *new* to *very old*.
5. In Sentence 5, change the number *two* to an appropriate number for a very old house.
6. In Sentences 6 and 7, change the color of the side of the house from *light yellow* to *white*. Change the color of the roof from *light gray* to *dark gray*.
7. In Sentence 8, change the phrase *many flowers* to *some small bushes and trees*.

Writing Activity 4 Writing a Paragraph (Unit 2)

Read the paragraph and follow the steps below to create a new paragraph. Write the new paragraph on the lines provided.

EXAMPLE PARAGRAPH 90

A Desert Plant

[1]The cactus is an interesting plant. [2]It grows in the desert. [3]It likes very hot temperatures. [4]It does not need a lot of water to live. [5]Its leaves are spiky. [6]Many people grow this plant in their gardens.

1. In Sentence 1, change *the cactus* to *seaweed*.
2. In Sentence 2, change *desert* to *ocean*. Do the same in the title and also change *a* to *an*.
3. In Sentence 3, make the verb *likes* negative.
4. In Sentence 4, make the verb *does not need* affirmative.
5. In Sentence 5, change *spiky* to *long and thin*.
6. In Sentence 6, change *gardens* to *aquariums*.

_____

_____

_____

_____

_____

_____

_____

Writing Activity 5 Changing Nouns to Subject Pronouns (Unit 2)

Fill in each blank with the correct subject pronoun (they, she, he, or it) for the noun in parentheses ( ). Then copy the new paragraph on the lines below. Give the paragraph a title.

Susan Brown and Joey Chen are actors. (1. Susan and Joey) _____ have very interesting careers. Susan acts in plays in the theater. (2. Susan) _____ works in New York City. (3. New York City) _____ is the best place to work in the theater. Joey acts in movies. (4. Joey) _____ works in Los Angeles. (5. Los Angeles) _____ is an exciting city. (6. Film studios) _____ make lots of movies there. Susan and Joey are very happy with their jobs. (7. Susan and Joey) _____ would not do anything else.

_____

_____

_____

_____

_____

_____

_____

_____

_____

_____

_____

_____

Writing Activity 6 Changing Nouns to Object Pronouns (Unit 3)

Read the paragraph and follow the steps below to create a new paragraph. Write the new paragraph on the lines provided. Be sure to write a title for your paragraph.

[1]Jane and I moved into a new apartment last week. [2]We were very excited. [3]We moved many big things into (our new apartment). [4]I had a television. [5]We put (the television) in the living room next to the window. [6]Jane's brother helped (Jane and me) move our couch and chairs. [7]We told (Jane's brother) to put (the couch and chairs) in front of the television. [8]Finally, we moved in our beds. [9]It took a long time to bring (the beds) in. [10]Jane said she would move her bed alone, but her brother had to help (Jane). [11]Moving is a lot of hard work. I hope we do not have to move again soon!

1. Change all the words in parentheses into an object pronoun (*me, you, her, him, us, them, it*).
2. In Sentence 9, make the verb negative.
3. In Sentence 10, change the word *alone* to the phrase *by herself*.

Read the paragraph and follow the steps below to create a new paragraph. Write the new paragraph on the lines provided.

Life on the Farm

¹My grandpa is a very busy farmer. ²Every day, he gets up at four o'clock in the morning. ³He eats breakfast. ⁴Then he goes out to the barn. ⁵There he feeds and milks the cows. ⁶When he finishes, he feeds the rest of the animals. ⁷Then he works in the cornfields until noon. ⁸He eats a fast lunch. ⁹After that, he works in the fields again. ¹⁰In the evening, he eats dinner. ¹¹Then he feeds the animals one last time. ¹²Grandpa finally goes to bed at around nine o'clock. ¹³He certainly does a lot in one day!

1. In Sentence 2, change *every day* to *yesterday*.
2. In Sentences 2–13, change all the verbs to simple past tense. Be careful of irregular verbs!

Life on the Farm

Writing Activity 8 Sentence Combining (Unit 4)

Read the paragraph. It is missing three sentences. Combine the sentences that follow the paragraph. Use and, but, *or* so. *Then write the three new sentences in the correct place in the paragraph.*

Lars's New Career

Lars is studying nursing. (1.) _____

_____

_____

Lars also practices nursing at a local hospital. (2.) _____

_____

_____

He is not ready to do that yet. (3.) _____

_____

_____ Because of this, it will be easy for him to get

a good job. Then he can help as many people as possible.

Missing Sentence 1:	He has to go to school five days a week.
	He takes several classes every day.
Missing Sentence 2:	He helps with everyday work there.
	He cannot help with emergencies.
Missing Sentence 3:	Lars's grades are very good.
	He will graduate with honors.

Writing Activity 9 Changing Past Tense to Future Tense (Unit 6)

Read the paragraph and follow the steps below to create a new paragraph. Write the new paragraph on the lines provided.

A Memorable Vacation

[1]When I was thirteen years old, my aunt and uncle took me on a wonderful vacation. [2]We went to the Black Hills in South Dakota. [3]We did lots of interesting things. [4]We visited Mt. Rushmore and took lots of pictures. [5]We visited a place to mine for gold. [6]One night, we even ate buffalo burgers for dinner. [7]It was very exciting. [8]I made memories on that trip that I will keep for a lifetime.

1. In Sentence 1, change *When I was thirteen years old* to *When I graduate from high school this year.*
2. Change all the verbs in the paragraph to *be going to* + verb.

A Memorable Vacation

_____

_____

_____

_____

_____

_____

_____

_____

_____

_____

_____

_____

Writing Activity 10 Adjective Clauses (Unit 7)

Read the paragraph below. Three pairs of sentences are underlined. Combine each pair of sentences by using an adjective clause. Rewrite the paragraph with your new sentences on the lines provided. The first two sentences have been combined for you.

The Discovery of the *Titanic*

[1]There were many scientists and explorers. They searched for the *Titanic* for a long time. They finally found it in 1985. It was deep in the Atlantic Ocean. This water was too deep for humans to visit without protection. Scientists solved this problem. [2]In order to explore the wreck, they used a **submersible**. This submersible was **controlled** by people on the surface of the ocean. Explorers took pictures of the *Titanic* with the submersible. [3]They even brought things to the surface. These things were on the **sunken** ship. Because of these people's efforts, we now understand more about the remains of the *Titanic*.

a submersible: a vehicle that can go very deep underwater
control: to guide
sunken: covered by water

The Discovery of the *Titanic*

There were many scientists and explorers who searched for the Titanic for a long time.

Appendix 3

Peer Editing Sheets

Peer Editing Sheet 1 Unit 1, Activity 27, page 32

Writer: _____ Date: _____

Peer Editor: _____

1. In three or four words, what is the topic of the paragraph? (What did the writer write about?)

    _____

    _____

    _____

2. How many sentences did the writer write? _____

3. Does each sentence begin with a capital letter? _____ If not, which sentences need to be fixed?

    _____

    _____

4. Does each sentence have a period or question mark at the end? _____ If not, which sentences need to be fixed?

    _____

    _____

5. What is the longest sentence? _____ How many words does it have? _____

6. Do you see an error in any of the sentences? _____ If so, write one of the sentences here, but correct the error.

    _____

    _____

Peer Editing Sheet 2 Unit 2, Activity 21, page 64

Writer: _____ Date: _____

Peer Editor: _____

1. Where does the writer want to go? _____

2. What is one reason that the writer wants to visit this place?

   _____

   _____

   _____

3. How many sentences are in the paragraph? _____

4. Did the writer remember to indent the first line of the paragraph? _____

5. Does the paragraph have a topic sentence? _____

6. Write the topic sentence here. _____

   _____

7. Does the paragraph contain any adjectives? If so, write them here. _____

   _____

8. Do you have any questions about what the writer wrote? (Are there any unclear sentences?) If so, write

   your questions here. _____

   _____

   _____

   _____

Peer Editing Sheet 3 Unit 3, Activity 24, page 91

Writer: _____ Date: _____

Peer Editor: _____

1. What sport did the writer choose to write about? _____

2. Did you know about this sport before you read this paragraph? _____

3. Does the paragraph have a topic sentence? _____ If so, write it here. _____

_____

_____

4. How many sentences are in the paragraph? _____

5. Does each sentence begin with a capital letter? _____ If not, write the sentences that need

to be fixed here. _____

_____

6. Does each sentence have a period or question mark at the end? _____ If not, write the

sentences that need to be fixed here. _____

_____

7. Which sentence has the most adjectives in it? Write the sentence here and circle the adjectives.

_____

_____

8. Does every sentence have a verb? _____ If not, write one of the sentences that is missing
a verb here and add a correct verb.

_____

_____

9. If there is a compound sentence in the paragraph, write it here. Circle the connecting word.

_____

_____

10. Did the writer use any object pronouns? If so, write a sentence that contains one here. Circle the object

pronoun. _____

_____

11. Write another sentence about the topic here. (Write your own original sentence.)

_____

_____

_____

Peer Editing Sheet 4 Unit 4, Activity 20, page 115

Writer: _____ Date: _____

Peer Editor: _____

1. Who did the writer write about? _____

2. Why do you think the writer chose this person? _____

   _____

3. Can you find a sentence that tells where the person lived? _____

4. Write the topic sentence here. _____

   _____

   _____

5. Now circle the subject in the topic sentence. Underline the verb.

6. How many sentences are there? _____ How many verbs are there? _____

7. In general, it is not good to have the same number of verbs and sentences. If these two numbers are the same, this means that the writer uses subject-verb order and simple sentences too often. The writer needs to work on sentence variety. Suggest that the writer try to combine sentences.

8. Write a few of the simple past tense verbs here. _____

9. How many times did the writer use *was*? _____ *Were*? _____ Irregular simple past verbs? _____

   Simple past negative verbs? _____

10. Are there any compound sentences that use *but*? _____ If not, suggest two sentences that can be connected with *but*. Write them here.

    _____

    _____

    _____

    _____

11. Did the writer use any time phrases? If so, write them here.

_____

_____

12. Is there an additional piece of information about the person that you would like to know? Write a question about this information.

_____

_____

_____

_____

Peer Editing Sheet 5 Unit 5, Activity 17, page 137

Writer: _____ Date: _____

Peer Editor: _____

1. Is the first line of the paragraph indented? _____

2. How many *-ing* verbs can you find in the paragraph? _____

3. Can you find a sentence that has *and* or *so* as a connector? Write it here.

    _____

    _____

4. Does every sentence have a subject and a verb? _____ If not, write one of the incorrect

    sentences here. Then correct it. _____

    _____

    _____

    _____

5. Adjectives help make writing easy to see or imagine. Can you find a sentence that does not have any
    adjectives? Write it here and add two adjectives. Circle the two adjectives that you added.

    _____

    _____

6. Does the paragraph have any sentences that contain adverbs of manner? If so, write one of them here.

    _____

    _____

    _____

7. Can you find any spelling mistakes? _____ Write the misspelled words and their correct spelling below.

Misspelled Word   Correctly Spelled Word

a. _____   a. _____

b. _____   b. _____

c. _____   c. _____

d. _____   d. _____

8. What do you think of the content of the paragraph? Do you have any comments or suggestions for the writer? If so, write them here.

_____

_____

_____

_____

_____

Peer Editing Sheet 6 Unit 6, Activity 19, page 164

Writer: _____ Date: _____

Peer Editor: _____

1. What goal does the writer describe in this paragraph? _____

    _____

    _____

2. Check for these features: a. Is there a topic sentence? _____

                              b. Do all the sentences relate to one topic? _____

                              c. Is the first line indented? _____

3. What is the topic sentence? Write it here. _____

    _____

    _____

4. Check for mistakes with subject-verb agreement. If the subject is singular, is the verb singular, too? If the subject is plural, is the verb plural, too? If you find any mistakes, circle them.

5. Is it easy for you to understand the meaning of the sentences in this paragraph? _____
   If not, write a sentence that is hard for you to understand.

    _____

    _____

6. Does the writer have articles in every place where they are needed? _____ If not, add them
   to the paragraph.

7. Do you have any ideas or suggestions for improving the paragraph? _____

    _____

    _____

    _____

    _____

Peer Editing Sheet 7 Unit 7, Activity 19, page 186

Writer: _____ Date: _____

Peer Editor: _____

1. What is the writer's opinion about cooking food at home or eating in a restaurant? Check one.

    _____ Cooking food at home is better.

    _____ Eating in a restaurant is better.

    _____ Both options are about the same.

2. What is one reason that the writer gives for his or her choice? _____

    _____

    _____

3. Write the sentence here that tells you the answer to Item 2. _____

    _____

    _____

4. Does the sentence in Item 3 have a subject and a verb? _____ If so, underline the subject one time and the verb two times. If not, add the missing words.

5. Is the first line indented? _____ If not, draw an arrow to show that the line needs to be indented.

6. Does the paragraph have a complex sentence? _____ If so, write it below. If not, make a suggestion about combining two simple sentences from the paragraph.

    _____

    _____

7. Do you think this paragraph is too long, too short, or just right? _____

If you think it is too long, what information should the writer cut? If you think it is too short, what information should the writer add?

_____

_____

_____

_____

_____

8. Does the writer include adjective clauses in the paragraph? If so, write the clauses below.

_____

_____

_____

9. Do you have any suggestions for making this paragraph better? _____

_____

_____

_____

Peer Editing Sheet 8 Unit 8, Activity 21, page 207

Writer: _____ Date: _____

Peer Editor: _____

1. What is the writer's opinion about smoking in restaurants? _____

   _____

   _____

   _____

2. Do you agree with the writer's opinion? _____

3. Explain your answer in Item 2. _____

   _____

   _____

   _____

   _____

4. Check for these features: a. Is there a topic sentence? _____

                                b. Do all the sentences relate to one topic? _____

                                c. Is the first line indented? _____

5. What is the topic sentence? Write it here. _____

   _____

   _____

6. Are articles used correctly? Circle any errors with articles.

7. Was it easy for you to understand the language in the paragraph? _____ If not, write one

of the confusing parts (sentences) here. _____

_____

_____

_____

8. How many sentences does this paragraph have? _____

How many sentences do *not* have a verb? _____

9. Can you think of anything to make this a better paragraph? _____

_____

_____

_____

_____

_____

Peer Editing Sheet 9 Unit 8, Activity 27, page 211

Writer: _____ Date: _____

Peer Editor: _____

1. What is the writer's opinion about what to do in this case? _____

   _____

   _____

   _____

   _____

2. Do you agree or disagree with the writer's ideas? _____

3. Please explain your answer to Item 2. _____

   _____

   _____

   _____

   _____

4. Are all the verbs in the correct tense? If not, write a sentence here with an incorrect verb. Then make the correction.

   _____

   _____

5. Does every sentence end with the correct punctuation? _____ If not, put a circle around any incorrect punctuation.

6. Can you understand everything the writer wanted to say? _____ If not, write one of the unclear

parts here. _____

_____

_____

Why is this unclear to you? _____

_____

_____

_____

7. Can you add two or more interesting adjectives in front of two nouns? (Add them on the student's

paper. Draw an arrow to show where they should go.) What are your two adjectives? Use the Brief Writer's

Handbook (page 228) if you need help with the correct order. _____

_____

Index

Photo Credits